Collins *gem*

Meditation

Paul Roland

Paul Roland is a qualified counsellor and teacher of spiritual development. He has studied meditation, yoga, Buddhism and the Kabbalah and is the author of several books on meditation and other topics.

HarperCollins*Publishers*
Westerhill Road, Bishopbriggs, Glasgow G64 2QT

www.collins.co.uk

Devised and created by The Printer's Devil, Glasgow

First published 2002

This edition published 2004

ISBN 0-00-718883-8

Reprint 10 9 8 7 6 5 4 3 2 1 0

Photocredits
Anville © pp 13, 33, 35, 58, 65, 109, 126
Photodisk © pp 17, 18, 20, 35, 38, 40, 44, 48, 63, 65, 81, 86, 87, 89, 106, 107, 108, 109, 113, 119, 123, 126, 128, 130, 131, 132, 136, 137, 138, 140, 1411, 144, 148, 156, 162, 164, 181, 188
NASA © p186

Printed in Italy by Amadeus S.p.A.

Contents

Approaches To Meditation · 53

INTRODUCTION

The exercises in this book are intended for relaxation
and increasing self-awareness. However, if you have
recently experienced mental or emotional problems or
are taking medication you should seek professional
medical advice before practising meditation on your
own. The author and publisher accept no responsibility for any harm caused by or to anyone as a result of
the misuse of these exercises.

Those new to meditation should be reassured that
there is no need to feel anxious for any reason. You
are not going anywhere, other than inward for greater
self-awareness and peace of mind. During this journey
you are always in control. You are not dabbling in the
occult, or communicating with spirits. The only spirit
you are communicating with is your own Higher Self,
which is the loving, compassionate, all-knowing
source and centre of your being.

WHY MEDITATE?

> 'The gift of learning to meditate is the greatest gift you can give yourself in this life.'
>
> *Sogyal Rinpoche*

The standard definition of meditation as 'an act of reflection and contemplation' is inadequate to convey the serenity and sense of detachment that can be experienced when the body is relaxed, the restless mind is at peace and one enjoys a blissful state of being which the Buddhists describe as being 'in the world but not of it.'

But meditation is not merely a method for achieving peace of mind and deep relaxation. When practised regularly for as little as ten minutes a day it can have a profound and positive effect on our mental, emotional and physical health.

I have been practising, teaching and writing about meditation for more than twenty years and have seen how it has quietly transformed and enriched the lives of my students in many ways. Some took up meditation in the hope of alleviating stress and associated sleep disorders, others sought relief from minor ailments such as migraines, while a few had a vague notion that it might help to bring meaning to their lives. All of them benefitted in some practical way after only a few weeks of attending my classes. But they soon discovered that once meditation became a small but significant part of their daily routine they began to benefit in more subtle ways from what might be called the positive 'side effects' of meditation; increased concentration, clarity of

WHY MEDITATE?

- To experience its direct mental, physical and emotional health benefits

- To learn how to relax

- To relieve stress

- To improve concentration

- To achieve greater self-awareness

- To gain a clearer sense of purpose

- To enjoy a sustained sense of well-being

- To foster a more positive attitude to life

thought, a clearer sense of purpose, greater self-awareness and a sustained sense of well-being.

Who Can Benefit?

Contrary to popular belief meditation is not the exclusive preserve of religious ascetics or those who are 'spiritually advanced'. Neither is it necessary for practitioners to subscribe to a particular belief system. Meditation is

Meditation need not involve esoteric or 'exotic' trappings

often associated with the philosophies of the east and in particular Buddhism because these traditions have developed it as a spiritual discipline, but it is merely a state of mind, a natural way to tap the limitless potential of our Higher Self or True Nature and explore the inner life of the unconscious.

This book has been written as an introduction for those who are new to meditation and who may be wary of such abstract ideas as 'letting go', 'looking inward' and 'emptying the mind' as practitioners are often urged to do. My aim has been to demystify the practice, to strip it of its more 'exotic' trappings, which can be off putting for westerners, and to offer safe and simple techniques for deep relaxation, stress relief, increased self-awareness and ultimately, a glimpse of the greater reality that exists beyond our physical senses.

Meditation For Health

The development of biofeedback, an increasingly popular medical technique in which patients mimic meditation techniques for pain and stress relief, stems from the discovery in the 1970s that meditation can be used to control the involuntary physiological functions such as the heart rate and body temperature.

Everyday stresses can trigger psychosomatic disorders

It is generally accepted now by those practising an holistic approach to health, that when we are under stress or are worried we can unconsciously manifest symptoms such as eczema, migraines and muscle aches – which in some cases may be psychosomatic in origin. These types of conditions are difficult to cure with conventional medicines. In such cases, meditation can often restore the natural balance of chemicals in the body, revitalise the functions of the vital organs and strengthen the immune system by addressing the source of this 'dis-ease' in our psyche, rather than simply fighting the physical symptoms.

There is a wealth of clinical evidence to support the claims that meditation can reduce high blood pressure, improve circulation, control pain and reduce muscular tension. Even the most basic breath-control exercises have been found to be beneficial in alleviating minor ailments such as anxiety attacks and sinus problems, as well as asthma and cardiac arrhythmias by improving the circulation of oxygen through constricted passages. As a result of these findings an increasing number of General Practitioners are now encouraging patients with stress-related ailments, addiction and even terminal illnesses to take up meditation as a complement to conventional treatment.

ALL IN THE MIND

Contrary to popular belief, various scientific studies have confirmed that meditation has a measurable physical effect on the brain and body.

In the 1960s Harvard cardiologist Herbert Benson and researcher Robert Wallace of the University of California revealed that meditation has a greater physiological effect than conventional forms of relaxation. Subjects were shown to breathe at a significantly reduced rate which affected their heart rates and blood pressure as well as their production of lactic acid: this is the chemical associated with the fight-or-flight response. As a result practitioners exhibited less signs of stress and sustained this relaxed response for some considerable time after the meditation sessions.

Subsequently, Professor N. Lyubimov, one of the world's leading neuroscientists based at Moscow's Brain Research Institute, discovered that meditation creates a distinctive pattern of activity in the frontal cortex, which he describes as a state of 'restful alertness', resulting in significantly improved mental agility, concentration and memory retention.

Other tests have shown that meditation balances the right and left hemispheres of the brain which relate respectively to the emotional and intellectual processes, creating a more balanced personality and a state of well-being.

More recently, researchers at Stamford University in California compared 144 methods of relaxation and concluded that meditation was more than twice as effective as any other technique.

LOOKING GOOD, FEELING FIT

Regular practice can also be highly beneficial for our intellectual and emotional well-being. Visualisation exercises, which use the imagination to reprogram the unconscious, can dispel negative conditioning, help us to overcome fears and phobias, develop self-discipline, improve personal performance in sports, business and the arts,

HEALTH BENEFITS OF MEDITATION

- Alleviates stress-related complaints, e.g. sleep disorders, anxiety attacks

- Relieves minor ailments, eg migraine, muscular tension

- Aids relaxation

- Revitalises functions of the vital organs

- Strengthens immune system

- Restores natural balance of chemicals in the body

- Reduces high blood pressure

- Improves circulation

- Helps control pain

- Reduces muscle tension

- Evokes a sustained sense of well-being

- Helps overcome fears and phobias

- Lowers hormonal activity, leading to a healthier and fitter body

- Fosters a positive attitude

- Offers a clearer sense of purpose

cultivate self-confidence and create a more positive attitude to life in general.

It has also been shown that meditation can lower hormonal activity in the body so that those who practise it on a regular basis look healthier and feel fitter than those who take up more physical forms of exercise.

The Roots Of Meditation

Contrary to popular belief, meditation is neither alien to our culture, nor to our nature. Although it is impossible to be certain where and when it evolved, it is fair to assume that primitive man took the first step towards self-awareness when he began to wonder where he had come from and what purpose there might be in existence.

By the 4th millennium BCE (Before the Christian Era) passive contemplation and nature worship had developed into a clearly defined spiritual discipline focussed upon a multiplicity of gods. Egyptian initiates into what were known as 'The Mysteries' (occult philosophy) sought to awaken their own divine qualities by 'assuming the god form', as it was known, of the mythical deity who symbolised the particular attribute that they required. While in the East, meditation formed the basis of yoga as a means of attaining complete control over the physical body and mind realising the True Self.

KABBALAH

The earliest form of structured meditation is thought to be a technique known as Merkabah ('rising in the Chariot'), a practise dating from the biblical era in which the worshippers heightened their awareness of the inner worlds using visualisations. These exercises form the basis of the mystical teachings known today as Kabbalah.

Kabbalah states that everything in the universe, including ourselves, is an expression of its Creator and that once we understand our true nature we will

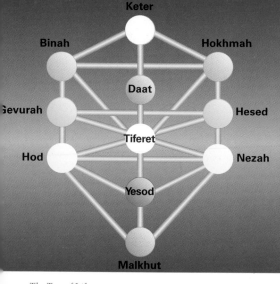

The Tree of Life.
The points on the Tree represent:
the Crown (Keter); Wisdom (Hokhmah), Mercy (Hesed),
Eternity (Nezah), Malkhut (Kingdom), Glory (Hod),
Judgement (Gevurah), Understanding (Binah), Foundation
(Yesod), Beauty (Tiferet), and Higher Knowledge (Daat).

understand the mysteries of existence. This heightened state of self-awareness, equivalent to the Buddhist's state of Enlightenment, is to be attained by exploring a central symbolic glyph known as the Tree of Life through guided visualisations known as pathworkings (see p. 170).

The Tree of Life serves as both a map of the human psyche and of the structure of existence, as Kabbalah envisages that human beings are in essence a world in miniature (microcosm).

THE ESSENES

Merkabah is thought to have been central to the spiritual disciplines developed by ascetic Jewish sects known as the Essenes and the Nazarenes of whom Joshua Ben Miriam (Jesus) is believed to have been a member. The Essenes established a community at Qumran where the Dead Sea Scrolls were discovered and there practised a form of yoga in which they sought to harmonise the seven complementary attributes of the Earthly Mother and of the Heavenly Father which roughly corresponded to the chakras of the Hindu tradition (energy centres believed to be situated between the base of the spine and the crown of the head). In practise this involved meditations on a symbol also known as the Tree of Life whose seven branches stretched heavenwards and whose seven

roots reached down
into the earth with
the human body
representing the
trunk which was to
be a channel for the
terrestrial and
celestial forces.

AWAKENING OUR TRUE NATURE

One of the aims of
meditation is to
transcend the
mundane
preoccupations of
the conscious mind
or ego, which has its reality in the physical world of
the five senses, and attain a heightened awareness of
our True Nature which is known variously as the
Higher Self, Christ Consciousness, Buddha Nature or
Soul. When we attain this altered state of
consciousness it is said that we will experience
supreme understanding, profound peace and a unity
with all things which is known as Enlightenment.

Meditation offers the means by which we can still the

restless, chattering conscious mind so that we can
hear this still, small voice within. Each tradition has
developed different techniques for achieving this
altered state.

MANY PATHS TO PEACE

Yogic, Sufi and Judaeo-Christian meditation has
tended to concentrate on various forms of heightened
concentration in which the individual seeks total
absorption in a single object or idea, while the
Buddhists seek to understand the nature of
consciousness through passive observation of the
mind.

But such distinctions are largely academic. In
practice, traditions and techniques are freely and
eagerly adapted in the shared search for greater self-
awareness and spiritual enlightenment.

CHRISTIAN TRADITION

Since the spread of Christianity Western orthodox
religion has often confused meditation with quiet
contemplation or prayer, seeing the practice as a path
to mystical consciousness reserved exclusively for the
mystics of the esoteric tradition. And yet, the early
Christians practised meditation in much the same
way as we do today. An early text, the *Philokalia*,

gives specific instructions for centring the heart, mind, breath, word and intent upon a single purpose.

> 'Collect your mind, lead it into the path of the breath, along which the air enters in, constrain it to enter the heart together with the inhaled air and keep it there. Keep it there, but do not leave it silent and idle. Instead give it the following prayer; Lord Jesus Christ, son of God, have mercy on me.'

Whichever technique you adopt you will find what is true for you in the silence and serenity of meditation.

Modern Christian prayer practice differs from that used in the early Church

THE BUDDHIST TRADITION

In Buddhism there is no distinction between sacred and secular life; every action, every breath is a meditation. Meditation is not seen as something to be worked at or perfected, but as an act of 'letting go' as we slip into a state of mind as effortlessly as we sink into sleep. The modern Buddhist master Sogyal Rinpoche, author of *The Tibetan Book of Living and Dying*, describes this act of release from worldly cares as being spacious and at ease. 'Slip quietly out of the noose of your habitual anxious self and relax into your true nature.' He says that once we should not try and possess peace of mind, but rather to remain in a state of 'calm abiding'. Intrusive thoughts should be considered as transient and insignificant as ripples on the surface of a lake. In such a state negativity, aggression and confusion can not exist and so no longer have a hold over us.

ZEN BUDDHIST TECHNIQUES

In contrast, a form of Zen Buddhism known as Rinzai ('sudden') seeks to silence the chatter of the conscious mind by confounding it with an enigmatic riddle known as a 'koan'. A typical koan asks, 'what is the sound of one hand clapping?'

Such riddles might seem abstract to the rational western mind, but the idea is simply to shock the

mind into a state in which perceptions and values are rendered meaningless in order that the practitioner can accept a new reality. Zen does not ask its practitioners to find meaning in life, but rather accept that life is merely a moment of being.

A very different approach is practiced by followers of Soto Zen, which offers a method known as 'Serene Reflection'. This involves sitting in silence and allowing the mind to settle like silt that has been stirred up in a muddy pool. Once this state has been attained acute awareness, and ultimately enlightenment, are said to follow naturally.

MEDITATION & YOGA

In the Hindu tradition the physical postures and
exercises of yoga are considered to be a form of
meditation in action, but there are also less active
forms of yogic meditation known as Dhyana and Laya
yoga. The latter seeks to stimulate the chakras using
visualisations in which the practitioner imagines these
subtle energy centres as blossoming lotus flowers of
varying colours. In Dhyana yoga there are two
approaches.
Either total
absorption is
sought in an
abstract idea or
the mind is
focussed on an
object, mantra or
symbol to the
extent that all
sense of physical
reality is rend-
ered meaningless.

*Yoga postures, or
asanas, are a
form of meditation,
in Hindu tradition*

TRANSCENDENTAL MEDITATION

Transcendental Meditation, commonly known as TM, is one of the most popular forms of meditation practised today. It was introduced to the West in the 1960s by the Mahresh Mahesh Yogi, who was then The Beatles' personal guru, and it quickly captured the imagination of the 'flower power' generation who were looking to the East for answers.

TM differs from other forms of meditation in that it requires practitioners to adopt a personal mantra (a sacred word or phrase to be repeated silently during meditation) and it also places great emphasis on the personality of the Mahreshi as the divine leader of the movement.

There are currently four million practitioners of TM world-wide including celebrities Arnold Schwarzenegger, Sylvester Stallone, Clint Eastwood and Elizabeth Taylor as well as international sports personalities and business executives who all claim to have experienced tremendous psychobiological benefits.

It is claimed that one hundred major Japanese multi-national corporations, including Sony, have integrated TM into their training programmes and have recorded a significant fall in absenteeism and an increase in individual performance.

Such claims appear to be backed up by the international journal *Psychosomatic Medicine* which monitored 2000 practitioners of TM over a five year period and concluded that they required less medical treatment; specifically 87 per cent fewer hospital-isations for heart disease, 55 per cent fewer for tumours, 87 per cent fewer for nervous disorders and 73 per cent fewer for lung, throat and nose complaints.

In the following chapters I have outlined hints and tips for meditation together with a number of different types of exercises that I have found to be particularly effective, so that you can discover the value of meditation for yourself.

> What really matters is not just the practice of sitting but far more the state of mind you find yourself in after meditation. It is this calm and centred state of mind you should prolong through everything you do.
>
> *Sogyal Rinpoche*

HOW TO MEDITATE

> When you meditate there should be no effort to control and no attempt to be peaceful. Do not be overly solemn, or feel that you are taking part in some special ritual. Let go even of the idea that you are meditating. Let your body remain as it is and your breath as you find it.
>
> *Sogyal Rinpoche*

Establishing The Habit

It can be difficult initially for westerners to establish the pleasantly addictive habit of meditation as we are conditioned to believe that we must be constantly active and productive. Setting aside time for ourselves for meditation is still considered by many to be self-indulgent and even somewhat eccentric.

- The first step in overcoming this inner resistance is therefore to accept that our mental and emotional well-being is as important as our physical health and that we owe it to ourselves to take time out to create space in which to sit in silence and still the mind.

- The second step is to establish a regular routine by
  deciding to set aside between ten or twenty minutes
  every day rather than wait for a convenient time
  because otherwise there will always seem to be
  something that needs doing more urgently than the
  meditation.

Creating The Right Atmosphere

You can encourage
yourself to meditate by
creating a tranquil
atmosphere and a sense of
sacred space in a corner of
your bedroom or study
with candles, crystals,
incense, fresh flowers and
appropriate ornaments
such as statues of Buddha,
inspirational pictures or
angels. In time this area
will become 'charged' with
your positive mental
energy and a sense of
peace, making it ideal for

quiet contemplation. Or you could create a healing sanctuary in a spare room and dedicate each meditation session to sending healing energy to those in need. This type of active meditation is an effective way to channel the emotional energy that is often stirred up whenever we are bombarded by images of suffering on the TV news and it helps to raise our consciousness from brooding on suffering to compassion.

PRACTICAL TIPS FOR CREATING YOUR OWN SACRED SPACE

- Be selective in choosing inspirational objects and pictures. Clutter is not conducive to concentration. A single central object should be your focus. If your room looks like a New Age jumble sale it will prove a distraction and defeat the object of the exercise.

- A small vase of flowers or a pot plant is an ideal focal object for meditation and a reminder of the eternal cycle of growth, death and rebirth in the natural world.

- It might be helpful to have a reminder of the primary principles governing the universe in the form of two candlesticks representing form and force, male and female, active and passive etc. The four elements of fire, air, water and earth could also be symbolised by objects with Earth represented by a plant or crystal; Air by incense, with a candle and a bowl of water representing the remaining elements.

- If you use candles take particular care as you will have your eyes closed for up to twenty minutes during meditation and you do not want to be distracted by intrusive thoughts concerning fire safety. So ensure that they are secure and that the holder is set in a bowl of water in case of an accident.

- If you are using candles or incense the room should be well ventilated as these consume oxygen and can lead to drowsiness and headaches.

- Not everyone responds to sitting in silent reflection for long periods of time so consider the use of a cassette or CD player as appropriate music, recorded visualisations and natural sounds can be very helpful in creating a conducive atmosphere.

CD recordings of natural sounds can be helpful in preparing to meditate

PLEASE
DO NOT DISTURB
Thank You!

- Whatever room you dedicate to meditation you will need to ensure your peace and privacy. If there are other people in the house or flat let them know in advance that this is to be a time when you are not to be disturbed and put a note to that effect on the door. Finally, before each session take the phone off the hook or switch on the answering machine.

PRACTICAL HINTS FOR GOOD PRACTICE

- It could be very helpful to record your experiences after each session, so consider keeping a diary in which you can describe the images that arise as these may have a symbolic

significance that you can then analyse at a later date.

- It is a good habit to take a shower before meditating as this is said to cleanse the aura (or energy field around the human body) of emotional residue as well as atuning the body. Bathing also makes us mindful of the body and impresses the importance of meditation on the unconscious. It is for these reasons that cleansing became a significant element of both esoteric and religious ritual.

- It can be beneficial to begin each session with a few gentle stretches to dissolve any tension and make the body supple in preparation for deeper relaxation. To do this:
  1. rotate the head gently from left to right and back again;
  2. then move it forwards and backwards

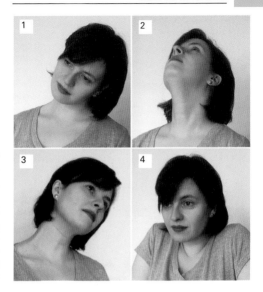

3. before finishing with a few side movements, titling your right ear to your right shoulder then doing the same with the left.
4. Finally raise both shoulders as high as you can, tense the muscles, hold for a few moments and relax.

- It is also a good idea to keep a glass of water beside you as it will help to ground you after you return to waking consciousness. (For an explanation of grounding and why it is necessary, see p. 77.) A cold, refreshing drink impresses on the unconscious the idea of flushing out impurities. You may also find it of practical use as the  throat can become dry during prolonged meditation and a cough can become irritating and distracting if you don't have something to relieve it.

- Try to avoid eating an hour before meditating as it can be difficult to attain a sense of detachment if your body is busy digesting a heavy meal.

- You may find it helpful to record the scripts and descriptions of the longer and more detailed visualisations as they can be difficult to memorise, although with practice it will be sufficient to recall the general outline of the exercise. The details of the inner journey will be impressed upon your unconscious.

- If you feel uncomfortable at any time during an exercise all you have to do is count down slowly from ten to one and open your eyes. Usually the anxiety has gone before you get to one and so you can resume the meditation. It is perfectly normal to feel apprehensive at times when you begin a programme of self-examination such as this as the ego resents having its pleasurable distractions taken away and being forced to sit in silence. The ego is not called the Inner Child for nothing.

POSTURE

As with other forms of relaxation and physical exercise it is important to establish good habits from the beginning, especially those concerning correct posture.

LYING DOWN

Many of the
exercises in this
book can be
performed either
seated or lying
down. If you prefer
to lie down on a mat
or bed use a cushion
to support your
neck. Your arms
should be by your
side and your legs

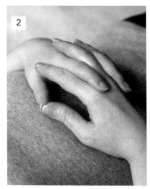

straight with the feet slightly apart (see fig. 1, p. 42). You might prefer to place your hands over your solar plexus (at your lower stomach, below the navel) to concentrate energy at this crucial energy centre. If so, form a bowl shape with your fingers entwined and your thumbs touching (see fig. 2, p. 42).

SITTING

If you prefer to be seated, place your feet flat on the floor and slightly apart in parallel with your shoulders. Your hands can be cupped in your lap as described above or placed palms down on your knees. Keep your spine straight. Your legs should make a right angle at the knee. If your legs are short, place a couple of books beneath your feet.

Keep your head erect as if you are looking straight ahead. Don't let your chin drop onto your chest because it will restrict the flow of air.

CLASSICAL POSTURES

It is not necessary to adopt the traditional postures of Yoga and Buddhism although these positions are intended to align the spine in preparation for channelling energy from the base of the spine up through the energy centres (chakras) to the crown. See page 29 for examples of Yoga positions, or *asanas*.

The half lotus position

To assume the full lotus position, place the right foot on the left thigh and the left foot on the right thigh. With the half lotus the right foot should rest on the left thigh while the left foot is tucked under the right thigh, or vice versa. The quarter lotus requires one foot to lie under the opposite thigh while the other foot is held under the opposite leg.

Alternatively, try a traditional Japanese posture by resting on your heels with a cushion supporting your bottom. In any position you may have to build up gradually the length of time you can sit.

Basic Breath Control

Focussing on the breath is one of the most effective methods of settling the mind and reducing stress. Once you can become mindful of the breath to the exclusion of all else and observe your thoughts with detachment then you will be ready to move on to more advanced exercises such as Creative Visualisation and Pathworking. Breath control is also essential for channelling and circulating healing energy around the body.

1. Close your eyes and sense the movement of your breath. Become aware of the rhythm and the rise and fall of your chest. (See fig. 1, p. 46.)

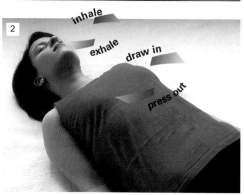

inhale

exhale

draw in

press out

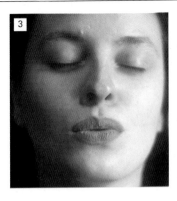

2. As you inhale press your diaphragm out then
   exhale while drawing the diaphragm in (see figure
   2, p. 46). This is the opposite movement to that
   which we usually perform involuntarily, but it will
   improve the circulation of oxygen throughout the
   body. It will also prove more relaxing as it is
   difficult to become tense and to experience a
   tightness in the chest associated with stress when
   breathing from the diaphragm rather than
   breathing in the chest as we usually do.

3. Next take a deep breath, hold it for a count of four,
   then let it out gradually until every last particle of
   stale air has been expelled. (See fig.3, above.)

4. Now begin to establish a regular rhythm inhaling and exhaling for a count of four with a pause for a count of two between each breath. With practice you will find a sense of detachment and serenity in this pause between the breaths when the body too appears inactive.

5. If counting is too abstract or boring you can use a mantra (a sacred word or phrase) or a simple affirmation such as 'calm and centred'.

6. Focussing on the breath is a form of silent meditation and much more difficult and demanding than one might imagine. So be patient with yourself and do not be discouraged if you become distracted in the beginning. When intrusive

thoughts arise don't try to suppress them but
observe them with detachment as if they were
birds flitting across the clear sky of your mind and
then bring your mind gently back to the focus of
your meditation.

Active & Passive
Meditation

Breath control is a form of passive meditation, which
requires that you sit still, allow the mind to settle and
enter a state of deep physical relaxation and
heightened awareness. In contrast, active meditation
requires us to observe the mind and body as we go
about our daily lives treating every act as a meditation,
no matter how mundane. It could be washing up or
preparing vegetables.

OBSERVING THE BODY IN ACTION

Active meditation trains the body to be productive
with the minimum of effort, to conserve vital energy
whilst remaining mentally alert.

To evaluate how economical you are in using vital
energy, try this simple exercise every day for a week.

EXERCISE

- At random moments during the day become aware of your posture and your physical movements.

  Are you constricting the flow of energy by sitting awkwardly? Do you waste a lot of energy fidgeting or pottering around the house or office simply because you find it difficult to sit still? Are you tense?

If so, do one of the simple head to toe relaxation exercises that you will find elsewhere in this book and get the energy flowing freely again (see Chapter 3.)

Train yourself to observe your body in action. Relaxation exercises can help ease stress and tenseness.

Do you indulge in mental chatter to fill the silence?

If so, take a breath and still the small talk for only in silence can we hear the inner voice that gives us guidance, insights and the answers we seek.

OBSERVING THE MIND IN ACTION

The first significant step to self-awareness is to establish the habit of observing what is known as the ordinary mind, or ego. The ordinary mind continually undermines our productivity, creativity and personal growth by indulging in idle daydreaming, self-criticism and regrets over past mistakes, but we can rein it in and train it to concentrate on the task in hand.

EXERCISE

• As with the previous exercise, observe your thought processes at random points during the day for a week or so.

Do you find yourself indulging in self-criticism over past mistakes? Do you fantasise about the future (perhaps you want to write a book, or cut down your hours at work), but do nothing to bring that reality into being? Become aware of when you are concentrating and when your mind wanders. When you become unfocused bring your mind gently

back to the task in hand as you would a pet that has
strayed from the path. Overcoming such problems is
simply a case of a lack of control over your thought
processes.

The ordinary mind habitually clings to the physical
world and the familiar thought patterns like a stylus in
a scratched record. But if we could focus our limitless
mental energy like a laser in the supercomputer that is
our brain we would be capable of unimaginable feats
and humanity would take a quantum leap in its
evolution.

APPROACHES TO MEDITATION

> If the mind is not contrived, it is spontaneously blissful, just as water, when not agitated, is by nature transparent and clear.
>
> *Traditional Tibetan saying*

Meditation can be difficult for beginners who often find that sitting in silence and emptying the mind is not as simple and easy as they had imagined. Our brains are a form of electrobiological supercomputer that are constantly processing innumerable streams of thoughts which can't simply be switched off at will. The first step in meditation is therefore to train the mind to be still and observe your thoughts with detachment.

Quietening The Mind

We can't control our thoughts, only our response to them. If we try to suppress them we will attach a significance to them and become distracted with the result that our thoughts will control us.

EXERCISE:
QUIETENING THE MIND

1. Make yourself comfortable, close your eyes and
   establish a relaxed and regular rhythm of breath
   control (see p. 45).

2. Now let go of all thoughts and immerse yourself in
   silence. Don't think about how long you will
   meditate for and don't anticipate having any
   visions or extraordinary experiences. Just enjoy the

stillness. Sustain this blank canvas in your mind for as long and as effortlessly as possible. If thoughts arise, note their passing but attach no significance to them.

3. When you are ready, open your eyes and return to waking consciousness.

Be assured that everyone experiences a degree of frustration when they first begin to meditate. As with most disciplines, from learning to swim to playing a musical instrument, it becomes easier with practice.

How did you find that first step? More difficult than you thought it would be? Was it difficult to sit still? Were you distracted by idle thoughts?

If you were plagued by thoughts of what you could be doing instead of meditating, stay with it and before long you will happily postpone your chores in order to mediate as it can become pleasantly addictive.

Starting Simple

The following exercises form the basic building blocks of meditation. Choose one and practise it once or twice a day for six days, then rest for one day before moving onto the next exercise. Once you can retain the images in your mind for at least five minutes, begin to explore other techniques described in the following pages, but feel free to return to these simple initial exercises whenever you want to develop your powers of concentration, or you need a break from the demands of the day.

EXERCISE:
ENTERING THE CIRCLE

1. Make yourself comfortable, close your eyes and when you feel suitably relaxed imagine a small white spot in the darkness.

2. Now visualise it growing larger as it draws nearer. Sustain the shape and the purity of the colour white as you watch it coming closer and closer until it is at arms length. It is now the height of a door and you are able to step into it. What do you see on the other side?

3. At first you might not have any clear images, but you should feel calm and centred.

4. At this early stage of your practice it is sufficient to be able to visualise a simple shape and to sustain it without effort. Significant symbols and imagery from the unconscious will come with practice.

5. If, however, you wish to use meditation purely for relaxation and to improve your powers of concentration, then simply stay with the initial part of these starter exercises that are concerned with visualisation and manipulation of shapes and colours.

6. When you are ready, open your eyes and return to waking consciousness.

If you feel confident, vary the exercise each time by visualising a coloured circle and see if you can sense the different qualities of energy associated with each colour.

THE CANDLE FLAME

This exercise has been practised for thousands of years by mystics and it continues to be a basis of modern meditation programs.

EXERCISE:
THE CANDLE FLAME

1. Light a candle and soften your gaze so that you are looking through the flame. When it is imprinted in your mind's eye, close your eyes and keep the image of the flame before you for as long as you can.

2. When the afterglow fades open your eyes and gaze at the flame again for a few seconds until you have fixed the image as before.

3. Once you have a sustainable mental image of the candle absorb yourself in the flame. This sense of becoming one with the object of the meditation is a primary aim of the practice and will help develop your ability to project your consciousness in preparation for more advanced visualisations such as pathworking.

4. When you are ready open your eyes.

EXERCISE:
THE MESSAGE

For this exercise you will need a pen and paper.

1. Make yourself comfortable with your back straight. Feet flat on the floor and slightly apart. Hands on your thighs.

2. Close your eyes and begin to focus on your breath. Take slow deep regular breaths. Expel the tension with every out breath.

3. And when you inhale breathe in a golden light which warms and calms you with every breath. Feel yourself relaxing with every breath.

4. Now imagine that you are writing your name at the top of the page. See it clearly.

5. What words, phrases or images do you immediately associate with yourself? Give yourself space to bring these words uncensored in from the unconscious.

6. Now keeping the channel open, so to speak, the inner ear alert and your sensitivity acute, open your eyes and write down all the words associated with yourself that come through.

7. Now close your eyes again and relax. This time imagine that you are writing the word 'Universe' at the top of the paper. See it clearly.

8. What words or images do you associate with the word 'Universe'? Give yourself space to bring these words in from the unconscious.

9. Now keeping the channel open, so to speak, the inner ear alert and your sensitivity acute, open your eyes and write down all the words associated with the word 'Universe' that come through.

10. Now close your eyes again and relax. See it clearly. Say any sacred name or prayer to yourself that you wish and begin to see your guide or guardian angel drawing near enveloping you with its wings or simply sense its presence.

11. This time imagine that you are writing the word guide, God or guardian angel at the top of the paper (whichever you feel comfortable with). What words or images do you associate with this word? Give yourself space to to bring these words in from the unconscious or listen for the whisper from within.

12. Now keeping the channel open, so to speak, the

inner ear alert and your sensitivity acute, open your eyes and write down all the words associated with your chosen word that come through.

13. Now close your eyes again and relax. Say any sacred name or prayer to yourself that you wish and again sense the presence of your guide or guardian angel enveloping you with its wings.

14. When you are ready imagine that you are writing the word 'Message' at the top of the paper. See it clearly.

15. Listen for the whisper from within.

16. Now keeping the channel open, so to speak, the inner ear alert and your sensitivity acute, open your eyes and write down the message that comes through.

17. Now consider the significance of what you have
    written. What conclusions can you draw from this?

Still Life

Contrary to popular belief, meditation is not solely
concerned with sitting in silence with the eyes closed.
One of its primary aims is to open our minds to a
greater reality in which we become aware that we are
one with everything in the universe and that our
apparent separation is an illusion. And we can only do
this with our eyes open.

The first step in developing this heightened state of awareness is practising what is known as a still life meditation in which the subject is a simple inanimate object.

Subjects such as an apple, stone or a vase are ideal and should be placed against a plain background so that you are not distracted by clutter.

MEDITATING ON AN OBJECT: SOME SUGGESTIONS

- Apple

- Stone

- Vase

- Candle

- Flower

- Mandala (opposite, second row left)

- Yin-yang symbol (opposite, second row right)

- Symbol for OM (opposite, third row left; see also p. 75)

- Statues or pictures of deities

- Religious or spiritual symbols, such as the Cross or Star of David

EXERCISE:
AT ONE WITH AN OBJECT

1. Establish a regular rhythm of breath control and relax. Say to yourself 'be at peace, be still.'

2. Don't study the object, simply observe it as if it was a bud that is about to blossom or an egg that is ready to crack open and reveal the new life within.

3. Become acutely aware of its colour, contours, texture and solidity as you become one with the

object. Imagine holding it in your hands then being absorbed inside it. As you do so you may find that the distinction between the object and the observer will become indistinguishable. If so, don't be tempted to analyse the feeling, just enjoy losing yourself in this sensation.

4. When you are ready, return to waking consciousness and open your eyes.

RELEASING TENSION

Having focussed on the breath and learnt to quieten the mind, the next stage is to increase awareness of the body.

When we are under stress we instinctively tense our muscles as part of the fight-or-flight response. This reaction is more obvious in people who grit their teeth, hunch

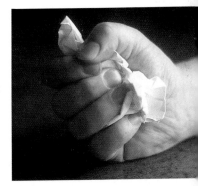

their shoulders, fidget or make a fist when under stress, but we all unconsciously transfer tension to our muscles to a certain degree and this can affect our health if we don't learn to relax and release this pressure.

The following exercise helps to achieve deep relaxation by identifying areas of tension and acknowledging this natural response to stress rather than fighting it.

It is particularly effective when practised in bed last thing at night and first thing in the morning to tone the body in preparation for the day ahead.

EXERCISE: BODYSCANNING

1. When you are comfortable close your eyes and become aware of the density and warmth of your body. You feel heavier with each breath and as you do so the warmth intensifies.

2. Now take a long, deep breath and expel all the stale air by making a soft 'F' sound. This controls the stream of air and helps to draw out the last particle of air from the lungs.

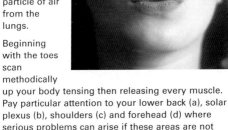

3. Beginning with the toes scan methodically up your body tensing then releasing every muscle. Pay particular attention to your lower back (a), solar plexus (b), shoulders (c) and forehead (d) where serious problems can arise if these areas are not regularly treated in this way.

4. Curl your toes (a), hold it for a moment, then relax.

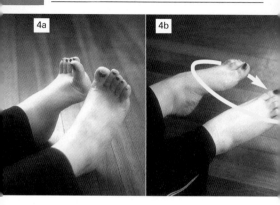

Make a small circle with your ankles (b) then tense
your feet and release. Clench the calf muscles in
the lower legs, then the thighs and the buttocks
before moving on to the lower back where you
should be able to sense a considerable amount of
tension. Release this tightness by drawing it in and
directing the warmth to that area. Visualise a soft
blue healing light massaging the muscles.

5. Now tighten the chest, hold for a moment and
relax. Then do the same with the solar plexus,
tightening, holding and relaxing. Can you sense the
warmth intensifying here? Feel it being absorbed
into the cells, tissues and muscles.

6. Next hunch the shoulders as high as you can, hold it there, then relax. (See fig. 6a, p. 71.) Move on to the upper then the lower arms. Tense them then after a moment relax. Now clench the fists and release. (See fig. 6b, p.71.)

7. Tense your neck and relax. Finally, pull a face to work those muscles and sense the tension draining away to be replaced by the warmth of the vital force that now saturates your entire body.

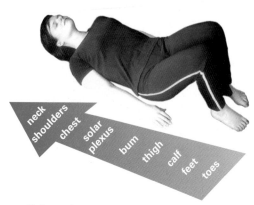

Body scanning

8. You may have thought you were reasonably relaxed before you began the exercise, but it is not until you scan the body in this methodical manner that you realise how tense you really were.

Mantras: The Sacred Science Of Sound

Since the earliest times sound has played a central role in religious rituals. The ancient Egyptians believed that the world came into being when Thoth, the God of Wisdom, uttered the sacred word of creation. This concept was subsequently adopted into Judaeo-Christian cosmology, with 'the Word' being the manifest expression of God.

Thoth: sound was as central to the sacred rituals of the Ancient Egyptians as it was to other major belief systems

'Words of Power' were also central to the world of the medieval magicians and are still used today as a focus for meditation by both eastern and western practitioners to still the mind and attune to a higher state of consciousness.

ABRACADABRA
BRACADABR
RACADAB
ACADA
CAD
A

Perhaps the best-known example of an ancient word of power: spoken or written as shown here, as early as the 2nd century AD 'abracad-abra' was believed to invoke great forces

The physical effects of these phrases, known as mantras in the Hindu and Buddhist traditions, were studied by the scientist Hans Jenny in the 1960s. They were shown to produce symmetrical patterns similar to certain Tibetan mandalas which are symbolic of universal harmony.

One of the most commonly used chants in meditation is the Buddhist blessing '*Aum mani padme hum*', which roughly translates as 'hail to the jewel in the lotus', an acknowledgement of our Buddha, or divine nature. But for practical purposes any word or phrase can be used to induce a serene trance-like state and can be intoned silently or aloud, although it is thought that when it is repeated aloud the vibration raises the frequency of energy in the immediate vicinity creating a rarefied atmosphere conducive to worship.

In the Buddhist tradition the sounds also have a mystical significance. 'O' is the sound of perfection and wholeness; 'U' symbolises the descent of spirit into matter; 'A' represents the intellect; 'H' is the sound of the breath of life and 'M' symbolises the interdependence of spirit and matter.

In the Tibetan tradition the three primary sounds on which most mantras are based are 'OM', the transcendent Universal Unity; 'AH' expressing the perfected human being and 'HUM', the individual striving for completeness.

GOOD VIBRATIONS

At some point in your practice you should try incorporating a mantra into your meditation to test its effectiveness for yourself. Westerners tend to feel uncomfortable when chanting aloud, but you should persevere with it for at least a week, if only to free yourself from feeling self-conscious, as one of the

MAKING A MANTRA

- Breathe deeply then exhale slowly and evenly as you chant your chosen word or phrase.

- You need to intone it as loudly as you can so that its vibration resonates in your chest.

- Try to establish a continuous flowing cycle of sound so that the end of a phrase blends seamlessly into the next.

- Maintain an evenness of intonation and rhythm so that the repetition becomes hypnotic.

- Absorb yourself in the sound and gradually lower the volume of your voice until it resonates within you. When you have attained this state, lose yourself in the vibration. Imagine yourself going deeper and deeper into your body and then into the essence of your being.

- When you are ready to return to waking consciousness count down from ten to one and open your eyes.

primary aims of meditation is to lose that sense of self. If you don't like the idea of chanting in a language that you are not familiar with, you could substitute a suitable word or phrase of your own choosing such as 'peace' or 'calm and centred'. Even repeating your own name can have a remarkable effect.

GROUNDING

Unless you are properly grounded there is a possibility that you may become what is known as a 'bliss junkie', a person who becomes addicted to the pleasant sensations that meditation can generate in which you attain a sense of temporary detachment from the real world. However, it is important to understand that meditation does not offer an escape from reality or one's responsibilities, but rather a heightened awareness of the world around us and our significance in influencing it for the greater good.

The other reason why you need to be grounded is that some people find themselves rocking back and forth during meditation because they cannot channel the excess energy that is released when the chakras are opened. Grounding earths this etheric electricity safely into the earth.

EXERCISE:
THE OAK TREE

1. Make yourself comfortable in a straight-backed chair, close your eyes and focus on your breath.

2. When you feel suitably relaxed imagine that you are resting your back against a huge oak tree. Allow the season and the setting to arise spontaneously as

these may have a symbolic significance that can be analysed later.

3. Sense the strength of this sturdy tree whose branches tower over you and be aware that it is supporting you as you snuggle against its trunk.

4. It has stood here for centuries and weathered the elements drawing its strength from the earth and its life force from the sun. Now you too will tune in to this energy as you sense yourself merging with the oak.

5. Visualise yourself sending fibrous roots of etheric energy deep down into the earth from the soles of your feet. These roots secure you to the ground and also serve to draw up energy from the earth to revitalise every cell of your being. Sense this energy rising through your lower legs, into your upper legs and on into your back.

6. Now imagine that you are raising your arms to the sky merging with the branches. Draw down the sunlight and with it the universal life force that nourishes all plant life. Sense the two streams of energy from the earth and the sky merging within you, stimulating the chakras and saturating every cell.

7. When you are ready return to waking consciousness by counting down from ten to one. As you do so become aware of your surroundings

and sense the weight of your body sitting in the chair. Then open your eyes. As you have been deeper in this exercise than before it is advisable to sit still for a few minutes before resuming your activities.

Visualisations: Activating Your Imagination

Children live in the world of their imagination where wishes can come true, wickedness is punished and goodness is rewarded. But when we grow up we turn our back on this inner world and awaken to the realisation that life is not as simple, nor Fate as fair as we once believed. We cease to believe in magic and instead become preoccupied with the reality and responsibilities of the material world. But in dismissing the imagination as a distraction and its imagery as nothing more than unproductive idle daydreams we are neglecting the most powerful means we have for transforming our lives.

Imagination is the key to the unconscious and the

means by which we can create our own reality. By using our imagination creatively in meditation we can erase negative conditioning (such as fears, phobias and feelings of inferiority) and reprogram the unconscious with positive life-affirming thought patterns that can remodel our self-image, improve our health and attract exactly what we need from life.

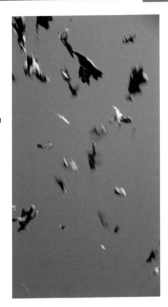

Visualisations, such as those described below, will help you to develop your imagination and focus your mental energy so that you will be able to enter and explore the inner reality of the unconscious at will.

EXERCISE: PROJECTING CONSCIOUSNESS

1. Make yourself comfortable, close your eyes and focus on the breath until you feel suitably relaxed. When you are ready, begin to picture your surroundings in as much detail as you can.

2. Now visualise yourself walking around the room examing each object in turn and occasionally looking back at yourself sitting in the chair.

3. When you can sustain this image for a few minutes walk through the door and go out into the street. Sense the fresh air on your face and the change in temperature. Listen for the sounds of the neighbourhood.

4. Then when you feel secure with this new perspective take a leisurely walk around the block noting the houses and gardens, the passing traffic and whatever you would normally see when you go for a walk. Don't rush through this exercise or skip any significant details as you might when day-dreaming. This is not a journey in the imagination but the first steps in learning to project your conscious mind beyond the confines of the physical body.

5. When you reach your home, walk through the front door and return to the room where you began. Count down slowly from ten to one, sense the weight of your body and open your eyes.

EXERCISE: REVIEWING YOUR DAY

As with the previous exercise, this visualisation trains the mind to remain focussed for a sustained period. It is also useful for improving self awareness and can help clear negative feelings such as guilt before they can become a potential source of disease. It will even help those who have had trouble sleeping.

1. Before you go to sleep each night close your eyes, breathe deeply from the diaphragm and repeat the phrase 'relax and recall, relax and recall' until you feel serene and centred.

2. Then begin to visualise the events of your day in detail beginning with the morning. You don't need to relive them. Instead watch them as you would a movie with yourself as one of the characters on screen.

3. How would you act differently if given the chance to play your part over again tomorrow? Don't be too critical of yourself or others. See any mistakes as opportunities to learn and improve. Perhaps you can now see more clearly why you experienced certain difficulties and appreciate why others reacted to you in the way that they did.

4. Watch as the screen goes blank at the end of your 'movie' and affirm that this day is now a part of the past. You cannot relive it. Let it go.

Mind Magic

Once you accept the possibility that you can create
your own reality you can make your imagination work
for you. All you have to do to make your dreams come
true is to visualise whatever you want and empower
those images with mental energy to create a blueprint
or thought form in the unconscious. If you can sustain
the image in meditation it will eventually manifest in
the physical dimension through the power of the Will.
This process is known variously as Creative
Visualisation or Active Imagination, the latter name
having been given to it by the Swiss psychologist Carl
Jung who considered it an effective tool for personal
growth. If you wish to test the potential of
Visualisations for yourself, follow the guidelines below.

To give your own visualisations the best chance of
success keep the following in mind.

- **The ideal subject for a visualisation is something for
which you have a strong desire and that you believe
you are capable of achieving, given the opportunity.**

  A visualisation will programme the unconscious to
  recognise and accept the opportunity when it arises,
  but only you can determine what you make of it after
  that.

- **You need to be willing to accept what you create or attract.**

This may sound strange, but even the most ambitious people can be unconsciously wary of success. They might doubt their ability to cope with the demands it makes upon them, or they might consider themselves to be unworthy in some way. Such  people will unconsciously undermine their own efforts. So, be honest with yourself when setting yourself goals and always ask yourself if you are prepared to accept the responsibility that it brings. This is particularly true if you wish to attract a new partner or improve a relationship.

- **Finally, your goal should be clearly defined**.

If, for example, you want a more satisfying job with

less stress and more time for yourself you need to
visualise yourself enjoying that lifestyle and imprint it
upon the unconscious with a simple, unambiguous
affirmation to that effect. Otherwise you may find
yourself in an opulent office working late every night
of the week to justify your employer's expectations or
driving an expensive new car that drains your
finances.

EXERCISE:
THE LIFE PLAN

Test the power of creative visualisations for yourself by
setting yourself a short term goal and seeing it
materialise in your imagination as described below.

1. Draw up a list
   of things that
   you want to
   achieve under
   the following
   headings:
   Work,
   Wealth,
   Lifestyle,
   Relationships,
   Self-expression,
   Leisure and
   Personal
   Growth.

2. Now choose one of these to meditate on at least once a day for a week.

3. Then make yourself comfortable, close your eyes and visualise your ideal scene. If your chosen theme was 'relationships' see yourself enjoying an improved relationship with your family, friends and colleagues at work, or a fulfilling relationship with a new partner. It is important that there should be sharing, consideration and unconditional love on all sides.

4. If you are visualising in the hope of attracting a new partner it is vital that you do not impose a face on that person, but picture instead a vague figure with the qualities that you require. If you fill in too many details, you risk attracting what you have wished for rather than what you need.

It is often the case that those who have experienced a series of destructive and difficult relationships can't break the cycle because they insist on projecting an image of their ideal partner on a partner who can't possibly live up to that image, rather than accepting that person as they are with all their imperfections and a will of their own. So, remain open and willing to receive whatever the Universe and your own Higher Self consider is right for you. And be ready to accept the responsibility that comes with it.

When you meditate it is important to see yourself
satisfied with your achievements, rather than simply
being successful and enjoying the material comforts. If
you focus exclusively on possessions and a life of leisure
you may get it, but it may come at the cost of your
peace of mind and your health. Your life should be
enriched by what you attract, not just your bank
balance.

EXERCISE:
THE MONUMENT

1. Make yourself comfortable with your back straight.

Your feet should be flat on the floor and slightly apart. Rest your hands on your thighs.

2. Close your eyes and begin to focus on your breath. Take slow deep regular breaths. Expel the tension with every out breath.

3. And when you inhale breathe in a golden light which warms and calms you with every breath. Feel yourself relaxing with every breath.

4. Imagine that you are inside a vast low-lit chamber which you sense is part of an even greater complex. Before you is a winding staircase to the ground floor. You descend the stairs until you come to the exit and once outside you turn back to face what is a giant hollow statue. It is a statue of yourself, a monument to your achievements and abilities, some of which have not yet been realised.

5. If this seems too incredible just imagine that we all construct these monuments to our achievements in our own inner world. And consider the fact that we have all done things in our lives of which we are justly proud, even if they eventually sink into the back of our conscious minds. Each life is unique and of value to those who love us and to those who watch over us.

6. Now you step back and look the statue over. Is it vast or modest? In good repair or neglected? What else do you note that is significant about its

appearance? Where is it? Perhaps it is at the entrance to a great harbour or city. If so, what is your immediate impression of the city? Is it a chaotic place, an intense hive of organised activity or a genteel old-fashioned town? Perhaps it is a rural setting or in a clearing in the jungle? What is the surrounding terrain like?

7. Are there any other people in the vicinity and if so, are they admiring your monument? Can you hear what they are saying about it or you? How do they react and how do you react to them?

8. You approach the base of the monument and read the inscription that summarises your life. What does it say?

9. Now open your eyes and note down everything that you can remember, starting with the inscription. When you are finished end the exercise by writing what you would have liked to have seen on the inscription. What do you want to be remembered for? How would you sum up your qualities and the aspects that you would like to improve upon?

INCREASING SELF-AWARENESS

The Chakras

There are believed to be seven major energy centres in the human body known as 'chakras' (from the Hindu word meaning 'wheel') which are traditionally depicted as spinning vortices of various colours.

Each colour has a symbolic significance so if we need to revitalise our body after an illness for example, we can stimulate the Sacral chakra which is the centre of physical energy by visualising the corresponding colour.

Alternately, if one of the chakras has become overdeveloped we can bring it into balance with the others using a similar technique. For example, an overdeveloped (or too open) Solar Plexus chakra will stimulate the emotions to such an extent that it will be difficult to make impartial decisions: you will be too emotionally involved.

During periods of stress the chakras can become drained of energy and disrupt the freeflow of the life

The chakras: Root/Base chakra (brown); Sacral chakra (red); Solar Plexus chakra (orange); Heart chakra (green); Throat chakra (blue); Brow chakra (indigo); Crown chakra (white)

force causing an imbalance in the body or dis-ease which will manifest as physical symptoms. So it is important to attune yourself to these subtle energy centres and to incorporate a balancing and centering exercise in your meditation routine.

EXERCISE: CENTERING THE CHAKRAS

This exercise stimulates the circulation of energy and creates a sense of well-being making it ideal for getting your day off to a good start.

1. Stand with your arms by your side, or sit as shown in the figure below, or with your feet flat on the floor, your arms by your side or with your hands cupped in your lap. Close your eyes and breath deeply from the diaphragm.

2. Begin by visualising a sphere of brown light beneath your feet. Sense the life force from this seventh energy centre, the Root or Base chakra grounding you in the earth.

3. Now visualise a second sphere emerging from the Sacral chakra beneath your navel. The colour of this sphere is red, the colour of physical energy. Feel the power of this energy centre surging down through your legs and up into your chest, back, arms and fingers.

4. Next imagine a third sphere radiating from the Solar Plexus chakra, the centre of the emotions. The colour of this sphere is orange. Orange stabilises the red of physical energy with the yellow of the

mental level. If you feel emotional as this chakra releases its energy don't suppress it. It is obviously a blockage that needs to be cleared. (See fig., p. 95.)

5. A fourth sphere now emerges from the Heart chakra in the centre of your chest. Its colour is green, the colour of harmony and of Nature. Stimulating this chakra cultivates compassion and creates a more positive, less self-centred perspective of life.

6. The fifth centre is the Throat chakra. It is to be visualised as a vivid blue sphere. Blue governs the passions and the mental processes and is symbolic of our ability to express our thoughts and feelings in speech and song.

7. The next chakra is on the Brow. Its colour is indigo and it governs intuition and wisdom.

8. Finally, focus on the Crown chakra as a pure white sphere of light and energy just above your head.

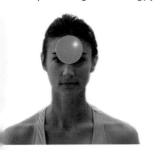

9. Now visualise each of these vibrantly coloured spheres aligned along the axis of your spine and sense how they are attuned to one another, balancing and centering the vital energy that maintains your health and sense of well-being. Watch as they merge into one another, rising in a stream of multicoloured light that overflows out of the Crown chakra into the aura, showering you in revitalising energy that cleanses and invigorates you from head to toe.

9. When you are ready, gradually return to waking consciousness by counting slowly down from ten to one and open your eyes.

CLOSING THE CHAKRAS

Always remember to close down the chakras. You can do this by visualsing each centre in turn fading like a light that is dimming or closing like the petals of a lotus flower. You can also pass your right palm over your body from the crown down as if to seal them

Spheres of Light

In both the western esoteric (non-orthodox) traditions and the philosophies of the East, human beings are considered to be a microcosm, or a universe in miniature. As such, we contain all the elements of the cosmos and the attributes of the Divine in finite form. If we wish to understand the nature of the universe and its creator we can examine the inner world of our own psyche using an advanced form of visualisation known as Pathworking (see p. 170)

In the Hindu tradition these Divine qualities are symbolised by the seven chakras and in the Jewish mystical tradition known as Kabbalah (which forms the basis of the western esoteric tradition) they are visualised as multi-faceted spheres of light known as the sephiroth. (See p. 21.) When superimposed on the

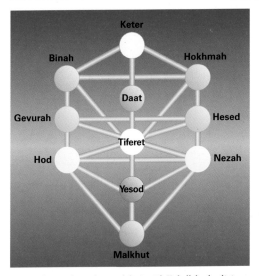

According to the tradition of the Jewish Kaballah, the divine qualities are symbolised in the sephiroth on the Tree Of Life.

human body the sephiroth are seen to roughly correspond with the chakras (see p. 92), while the limbs represent the governing principles of the active and passive pillars of Form and Force and the spine corresponds to the central Pillar of Equilibrium.

The central concept of the Kabbalah is that these complementary attributes should be in balance, both in the human body and in the world in which we live, otherwise imbalance will manifest as disorder and conflict in the world and as disease within the individual.

The following exercise offers the opportunity to experience the singular qualities of each sephiroth in turn on a physical and emotional level and it is also extremely effective in revitalising the body after illness or a stressful day.

EXERCISE: BRINGING THE SPHERES INTO BALANCE

1. Make yourself comfortable, close your eyes and focus on the breath. When you feel sufficiently relaxed begin by visualising a pulsating sphere of white light above your head. This is the source of celestial energy symbolised by Keter, the Crown sephirah.

2. Draw the light down into your head and sense the warmth dissolving all tension in your forehead and temples. If you suffer from migraine this aspect of the exercise is often enough to bring relief and can even cure the problem once and for all if practised on a regular basis.

3. Now sense the sphere of light in the middle of your forehead stimulating the Third Eye centre which is the etheric, non-physical organ of psychic sensitivity. As this opens you may experience a tickling sensation or you might see images which can be analysed after you return to waking consciousness. On either side of your head at this level visualise two gold coloured spheres. These are the sephirah Binah (Understanding) and Hokhmah (Wisdom).

4. Now visualise the light descending through your body stimulating each of the remaining sephiroth in turn:

(a) a blue sphere over the throat (symbolising Daat, the gateway to Higher Knowledge);

(b) the green coloured spheres of Gevurah (Judgement) and Hesed (Mercy) on a line with the heart centre in the middle of the chest and Tiferet (Beauty), symbolising the centre of the Higher Self;

(c) the sephirah of the intellect and the instincts, Hod (Reverberation) and Nezah (Eternity), as yellow spheres on either side of the solar plexus;

(d) then visualise a vibrant red sphere at the base of the spine symbolising Yesod (The Foundation), the centre of the worldly self or ego;

(e) and finally, imagine a brown sphere between your feet representing the physical dimension known as Malkhut (The Kingdom).

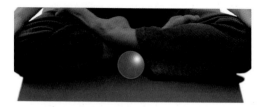

5. Visualise each sphere pulsating with the Universal life force and watch as they merge forming a shaft of multicoloured light energy through the centre of your body from the crown to your feet. You are now centred, reinvigorated and radiating with energy.

6. As you breathe in visualise this energy rising up into the Crown and as you exhale see it overflowing like a fountain of light down your left side. Now inhale and draw the energy stream up the right side of your body back into the Crown and as you exhale channel it down your spine to your toes.

7. When the energy is freely circulating exhale and visualise the light cascading from the crown down the front of your body. As you inhale draw it up behind you from heel to crown. Bathe in this

shower of light until you feel cleansed and in a state of deep relaxation.

8. When you are ready to return to waking consciousness close down the spheres one at a time by visualising them fading into your body and then open your eyes.

The Four Elements

We define ourselves by our likes and dislikes, our physical appearance, our personality and the identity that we were given at birth. But there is more to human nature than these qualities and characteristics. To understand our true nature we need to become acutely aware of other levels and elements that we are not conscious of, elements that reveal our place in the hierarchy of existence.

EXERCISE: INCREASING AWARENESS OF OUR PLACE IN EXISTENCE

1. Make yourself comfortable, close your eyes and focus on your breath. Consider your breath as the element of Air and the vital role it plays in the life cycle of your body. Become aware of how you restrict the flow of this vital force when you become tense, constricting the chest muscles with shallow rapid breaths and starving the vital organs of

oxygen. Resolve to establish a new habit of breathing from the diaphragm to alleviate stress and exercise control over your emotions.

Then expand your awareness to the natural world and consider the part played by all living things in replenishing the Air for the benefit of all life on Earth. Consider how dependent we all are for oxygen, one upon the other.

2. Now become aware of the skeletal structure supporting and giving form to your body. And see how the bones support the muscles, which facilitate movement. Consider your bones as the Earth element in your body.

Then expand your awareness into the natural world and visualise the part played by the soil. Minerals and rocks in supporting life, nourishing all creatures

with nutrients and protecting them from the weather. Visualise the hierarchy of nature from the wild animals in their caves and burrows to human beings seeking warmth and security in homes built from stone and cement.

3. Now become acutely aware of the blood circulating through your veins to maintain the flow of oxygen to the vital organs. This is the Water element of your being.

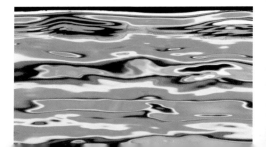

Then expand your awareness into the natural world and visualise the cycle of water that replenishes the plants and brings essential minerals to feed the land. Without water the world would be an arid desert incapable of sustaining life.

4. Next, sense that heat in your skin generated by the life force and consider this the Fire element of your being. Without the body's ability to regulate its own temperature, we would not be able to survive the fluctuating temperatures between night and day, or from season to season.

Then expand your awareness into the natural world and visualise the vital nurturing warmth and light of the Sun without which there could be no life on this planet.

5. Now become aware of the mineral element in your body, which maintains the chemical balance and nourishes the growing bones and muscles.

6. Then consider the vegetable element of your physical being, which regenerates the cells, governs growth and reproduction.

7. Next, sense the animal principle in the form of your mobility, vitality, instincts, social needs, cunning and curiosity.

8. Finally, raise your awareness to the level of your unique, human attributes – your memory, capacity for reflection and your imagination through which you

can raise your consciousness to the spiritual levels.

9. When you feel ready to return to waking
   consciousness, become aware of your surroundings
   and the weight of your body. Then open your eyes
   and stamp your feet to ground yourself.

House of the Psyche

The following exercise is one of the most effective
methods for raising self-awareness and revealing one's
current state of mind. The details will change subtly
but significantly every time you practise this
meditation, so it is worth keeping a diary of your
experiences to chart your development.

• Make yourself comfortable, close your eyes and
  breathe deeply. When you feel suitably relaxed
  visualise yourself standing at the gate of a house,
  which you are returning to visit after a long
  absence. Let the image arise spontaneously. Don't
  impose a picture on your mind or alter the details
  to fit what you would like to find.

• What kind of house is it? Large or small? Old or
  new? What state of repair is it in?

• Is the gate open and inviting, shut or hanging off
  its hinges? Is the surrounding wall, fence or hedge
  high, stable and substantial?

- As you enter and walk toward the front door, note the garden. Is it well tended or neglected? Is it a formal garden or a rambling, old-fashioned cottage garden? Is it infested with brambles and weeds, or is it mature and well cultivated? Are there soft pastel shades or vibrant coloured flowers?

- You arrive at the front door. Is it stiff or easily opened?

- Once inside, take your time and study the décor and the furnishings of each room in turn. Note any paintings or pictures.

- Go down into the basement and explore the boiler room, the bathroom and then the kitchen. What do you find there?

- Now return to the ground floor and go into the study where you will find a desk and a chair by the window. Sit down and open the envelope that has been left for you. What does it contain? Is there a letter, a photograph perhaps, or a small significant object? If there is a letter, it might contain advice on a matter that has been troubling you lately. Before you go, you feel the need to leave something of significance behind as a gift for the owner of the house. What do you leave here?

- Now retrace your steps and when you have closed the gate behind you, look back at the house. Has it changed in any way?

- When you are ready, return to waking consciousness and stamp your feet to ground yourself.

Self-Analysis

INTERPRETING YOUR SYMBOLIC IMAGERY

You don't need a degree in psychology to interpret the symbolic images in an exercise of this nature. Common sense, practice and experience should be sufficient to reveal their significance. But here are a few clues to stimulate the little grey cells and set you right at the beginning of your journey of self-discovery.

Weather

If you saw the house cowering under darkening skies, it suggests that you are reluctant to explore your feelings and attitudes at the moment, or that you are pessimistic by nature. But such doubts and anxieties can be dispelled as you gain confidence in your abilities. A sunny, cloudless sky indicates an optimistic attitude and a willingness to explore the inner worlds.

Walls, Fences, Gates & Doors

High walls and fences and stiff doors symbolise a defensive nature whereas gates and doors that readily open are indicative of a willingness to try new experiences and suggest that you expect little resistance to your ambitions.

The Garden

A neglected overgrown garden indicates that there are a significant number of issues to be resolved and that there has been a reluctance to subject oneself to critical self-analysis. There is also the suggestion that there is a tendency to neglect problems in the hope that they will solve themselves. If the garden follows a formal design then you prefer order in your life, but if it is a rambling cottage garden then you are more easy going and willing to let life take its course.

The colour of the flowers is also significant (see Chakra Exercise, p. 94) with vibrant colours symbolising an abundance of energy and strong emotions and pastel shades representing a preoccupation with the intellect and spiritual matters.

The House

If the house is old fashioned and in a good state of repair it suggests a conservative nature and concern with one's security and personal comfort. If it is modern then you are more likely to be open to new ideas and see all experiences as an opportunity for learning. If the exterior is in stark contrast to the interior it could suggest that you are concerned  with keeping up a facade to impress others or to protect your feelings.

According to Jungian psychology the cellar represents the instincts, the ground floor is symbolic of the impulses, instincts and fears of the unconscious mind, the upper levels represent the conscious mind and the attic represents the intellect and aspirations.

Pictures & Paintings

A painting is likely to be a revealing self-portrait, a symbolic image of your physical, emotional, mental or spiritual state or even a glimpse of yourself in a past life, so study it closely.

The Rooms

Each room has a symbolic significance.

In the **basement** you can expect to find a boiler representing the state of the bowels, a **bathroom** revealing your attitude to health, hygiene and privacy and a **kitchen** representing the digestion, appetite and your attitude to food.

A **dining room** symbolises family life and a willingness to share.

The **lounge** or **living room** represents your social life and attitude to friends and family.

A **bedroom** is symbolic of sanctuary as well as an expression of your sexuality.

Attics that feature a window on the world below represent our aspirations, but an attic crowded with junk indicates an unwillingness to let go of the past.

Finding The Right Path

When you are faced with a choice that could affect your career or a relationship it is often difficult to make a decision as your emotions can cloud your judgement. When you are confronted with such a dilemma use the following visualisation to clarify your thoughts and reveal which path is right for you.

1. Relax, close your eyes and visualise yourself beginning the day as if you had chosen option A. Commit yourself wholeheartedly to this reality. What are your feelings on awakening? Are you excited, anxious, secure or uncomfortable?

2. Visualise yourself having breakfast, going to work, socialising and returning home in this world. What problems might you encounter and how could they be solved? What support could you draw upon? If there are difficulties ask yourself if they are useful ones that you could learn from or are they obstacles to your personal development.

Would your pleasure and satisfaction be offset by unforeseen difficulties? Would this choice force you to live beyond your means, or compromise your ideals? Consider the practical aspects. Then consider your feelings. Would you be plagued by doubts, regrets or guilt, for example?

3. Now project yourself five years into the future and work through the day again. Then project yourself into the same situation fifteen years into the future and run through it again. Has the satisfaction lasted through the years? Has it been a good life? What was the cost of taking this path? What were the gains? But most important of all, did this life feel 'right' for you?

4. Now commit yourself to the alternative option and run through the whole process again. It should become obvious which is the 'right' choice for you in your present circumstances.

5. What could you learn if the path is a difficult one? Neither option will be problem free, or there would be no purpose in the experience, but one should feel 'right' for you and offer the greater challenge.

6. Now commit yourself mentally to the second path and follow that through in the same way.

7. Once you have made your decision, commit yourself to making the best of it. All paths promise

experiences that are of value, but if you change your mind and indulge in thoughts of what might have been you will make your journey more difficult than it need be.

Meditation Medicine For Mind & Body

Physical Ailments

Now that you have experienced the significant and lasting benefits of meditation for yourself, you can choose the exercises that fit your needs and incorporate these into your daily routine. But occasionally you may need to address specific issues that have not been covered in detail in the earlier part of this book. When you need to treat a particular ailment, or resolve a specific emotional issue, just dip into this section where you will find simple solutions to many problems that might be difficult to cure using conventional therapy and medication.

In the following pages are various visualisation exercises and techniques for addressing common physical ailments and also emotional disorders such as anger, fear and phobias. Further on you will find solutions for dealing with mental issues such as guilt, depression and stress, and finally, there are visualisations for exploring spiritual themes such as past life regression and how to ask for guidance on significant issues.

So, before you spend a fortune paying a professional therapist or relying on medication to pick up your spirits, help yourself the natural way.

Meditation is a simple and effective cure-all for many common ailments, particularly those that may be of a psychosomatic nature, such as migraine and eczema, as it addresses the source of the dis-ease in our psyche rather than simply alleviating the symptoms. By channelling the Universal life force to the origin of the ailment we can regenerate our cells and stimulate the body's natural defence system to fight infection.

SELF-HEALING

Ease into relaxation by focusing on the breath. Then begin by visualising a sphere of intense light above your head. Draw it down through the crown and sense its warmth irradiating every fibre of your physical being. Sense this energy being absorbed into every cell, saturating your bones, muscles, vital organs and skin until it radiates outward in an aura of multicoloured light. See the infection being burnt away in the intense heat of the life force leaving you in the centre of a sphere of light and impervious to re-infection.

If you are suffering from a tumour or another serious illness try supplementing the conventional treatment by adapting the above exercise to include a laser-like beam of healing energy destroying the malignant cells.

REVITALISING VISUALISATION

If you are recuperating after a long illness or simply want to wash away the dregs and negativity at the end of a long, demanding day, visualise yourself bathing in

a forest pool or waterfall. To feel the full benefit you will need to imagine the whole process in detail from divesting yourself of your soiled clothes to enjoying the cool cascading water gushing down the back of your neck and washing away the grime.

The more you can make the experience real, the more effective it will be. So, see if you can hear the birds singing, the motion of the trees in the gently caressing breeze and the warmth of the sun on your skin.

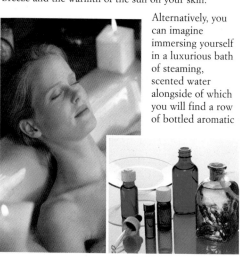

Alternatively, you can imagine immersing yourself in a luxurious bath of steaming, scented water alongside of which you will find a row of bottled aromatic oils. Each bottle contains a different coloured oil corresponding to a specific chakra. Which colour do you choose? Which chakra does it stimulate? Consider why you might have chosen this particular bottle.

SELF-DIAGNOSIS

The following meditation can reveal both the source of a symptom and what it might signify.

1. Lie flat on your bed, or a mat with a cushion to support your head. Close your eyes and take deep, regular breaths. In your own words ask that the source and significance of your illness be revealed to you. Then allow yourself to be taken on a journey through your body to the relevant place.

2. If you have difficulty visualising or sustaining the image, imagine a spec of light in the distance and allow yourself to be drawn towards it. When you have passed through the light you will find yourself in a symbolic landscape travelling either alone or with your guide. The landscape will eventually transform itself into a recognisable part of your body and at journeys end you will probably find something that symbolises your condition, or you may hear the voice of your guide revealing whatever it is that you need to know to alleviate the condition.

Body Awareness

It is a common belief among practitioners of holistic medicine that the psyche expresses 'dis-ease' by manifesting physical symptoms in 'appropriate' parts of the body.

The following exercises are designed to identify the source of many common psychosomatic ailments and address the underlying issues as well as alleviating the symptoms.

CHEST

This portion of the body contains the chakras governing the intellect (Throat chakra) and emotions

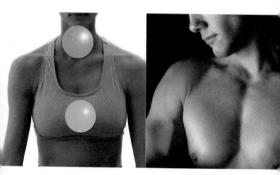

(Heart chakra) so a tightness in the chest or periodic aches and pains here suggests a tendency to indecision, particularly when there is an emotional issue confusing the matter.

MEDITATION

- Visualise yourself being giving healing by an angelic being who loves you unconditionally and who has been assigned to guide you and protect you throughout your life. Ask for their advice by stating that you need to know what is right for you at this moment in your life and bearing in mind the highest good of all concerned, so that you don't influence the answer by imposing your wishes and desires.

LOWER HALF OF THE BODY

This section contains the critical Sacral and Root chakras which can cause problems with the digestion and also undermine one's sense of security if they are allowed to become over- or underdeveloped. For example, someone who over indulges their emotions will be less able to make rational practical decisions and will cling to the past instead of searching for new and challenging experiences. They will tend to be self-centred, easily upset and unwilling to commit themselves to a relationship that requires responsibility.

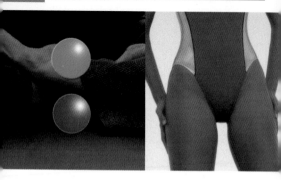

MEDITATION

- Use the grounding meditation (see p. 77) to impress a sense of security on the unconscious. It would also be beneficial to visualise yourself enjoying good health, a happy home life and the company of supportive friends and family.

BACK

If you suffer from chronic back pain and there is no obvious physical cause it can be the result of carrying more than your fair share of responsibility, or a burden that you are unable to bear.

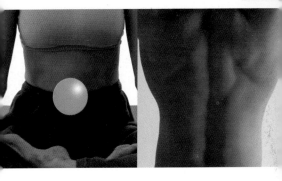

MEDITATION

- Establish the habit of breathing from the diaphragm to alleviate muscular tension in the lower back and release any repressed emotions in the Solar Plexus chakra. A helpful visualisation is to see yourself carrying a heavy sack of small stones up a steep hill which gradually becomes lighter as the stones trickle out through a hole to leave you with an empty sack by the time you reach the summit.

BLADDER

Bladder problems can be the result of a conflict

between the need to
control our emotions
and the urge to
express them freely.
Fear and anxiety can
exacerbate the
problem which
commonly originates
in early childhood.

MEDITATION

- Revisit scenes in
  your childhood in
  the company of
  your guide until
  you chance upon a
  significant incident
  that created the problem. Resolve the issue by
  visualising yourself as a baby cradled in the arms
  of your guardian angel who then sets you down on
  the Earth promising to be by your side throughout
  your life.

BOWELS

The inability to assimilate unpleasant experiences can
lead to chronic constipation, while impatience or an
over stimulated Solar Plexus chakra can result in

periodic bouts of chronic diarrhoea. More long term problems such as Irritable Bowel Syndrome (IBS) have become a common complaint in recent years as more and more people suffer stress generated by a gnawing fear that they are unable to control their own lives.

MEDITATION

- For chronic constipation visualise a sphere of intense white light above your head. Draw it down into your body and absorb the energy into your solar  plexus. Sense its warmth dissolving the tension in your abdomen and relaxing the muscles.

- For periodic bouts of diarrhoea imagine a sphere of intense white light at your feet. Draw it up through the soles of your feet into your legs and absorb it into your stomach. Feel the comforting warmth in your legs, lower back and stomach as you breathe deeply to calm the nerves that aggravate this condition.

- If you suffer with IBS, balance and center the chakras (see p. 94) as the likely cause of the problem is an over-active Solar Plexus chakra caused by a tendency to self-absorption.

EYES & EARS

Children in particular tend to suffer from eye and ear infections, conditions which can be psychosomatic as

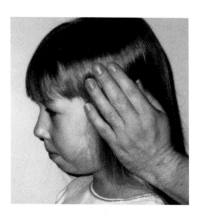

they unconsciously manifest a desire to 'turn a deaf ear' or a 'blind eye' to unpleasant facts, especially conflict in the home.

MEDITATION

- Sense the life force glowing in the palm of your hand, warming the skin. Now visualise yourself putting your palm to the infected eye or ear and see the energy being absorbed to where it can neutralise the infection. You can treat a child this way without its being present.

FEET & LEGS

If all physical factors have been discounted, aches and pains in the feet and legs could be symptomatic of an anxiety about being able to support oneself (literally to stand on one's own two feet). Or a fear of change as the body manifests an incapacity to 'move on' to new areas.

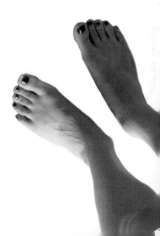

MEDITATION

- Try the projection of consciousness exercise on page 82, in which you see yourself leaving the room and taking a walk around the neighbourhood.

HANDS & ARMS

Crippling, restricting ailments such as rheumatoid arthritis can be symptomatic of the sufferer's desire to withdraw from the world and be dependent upon others to sustain and care for them. In such cases the source of the condition is often an irrational fear that the outside world is hostile and uncaring.

MEDITATION

- Visualise immersing your hands and arms in a basin of steaming warm liquid which gives off an intoxicating perfume. Watch as the liquid is absorbed into the skin, regenerating the affected cells and restoring suppleness to the muscles, tissues and joints.

HEAD

Migraine headaches are one of the most common psychosomatic ailments, but one that can be easily cured by regular meditation. The pain is often the result of unbearable pressure to resolve something that seems to have no solution creating a struggle between the head and the heart, the emotions and the intellect.

MEDITATION

- Visualise a sphere of intense white light above your head. Draw it down and absorb it into your head where it dissolves the pain.

SHOULDERS

If we believe we are shouldering too heavy a burden of responsibility it is possible to transfer that anxiety to the neck and shoulders.

MEDITATION

- Visualise yourself carrying your family on your back along a rocky path. Now set them down and watch as they amuse themselves, enjoying a picnic and playing together in the adjoining field. Affirm to yourself that you don't need to carry them through life. Attempts to control and overprotect your family will only exhaust you and prevent them

from assimilating the experiences they need from this life. Let go and let the angels watch over them. You just enjoy the moment.

SKIN

Eczema and other psychosomatic skin conditions are invariably symptomatic of a lack of self-confidence and of a distorted image of oneself which manifests as an unconscious desire for the sufferer to 'get out of their skin'.

MEDITATION

• Visualise yourself bathing in a scented pool and sense the warmth of the water saturating your skin with a revitalising essence. Indulge yourself for as long as you wish as the scented oils are absorbed into the tissues and muscles regenerating each and every cell. When you emerge from the water you

see that the oils have coated your skin with a protective layer making you impervious to the negativity of others.

PAIN RELIEF

It is a proven scientific fact that meditation can accelerate the healing process by stimulating the secretion of endorphins which are the body's natural painkillers. If you suffer physical, emotional or psychological pain the following visualisations should bring much needed relief.

MEDITATION

- Allow yourself to slip into a state of deep relaxation. Then imagine wrapping yourself in a warm, comforting blanket which begins to draw out the infection and the pain, soaking them up in the same way as a sponge absorbs liquid. Now snuggle into the blanket and luxuriate in the relief it brings. Detach yourself from the physical senses and drift

off to sleep in the soft, enveloping security of the blanket.

- Alternately you can imagine immersing yourself in a steaming bath of scented water which softens the knots in your tense muscles and saturates the tissues with healing energy. Visualise the affected cells as brittle crystals dissolving in the warm water.

- Other methods involve channelling the pain into a rock which disintegrates into dust to be blown away on the breeze. Or imagining that you are grounding the pain through a tree in the same way that a real tree would earth lightning during a storm.

Emotions

In recent years personal growth gurus (spiritual teachers) have been urging us to 'get in touch' with our feelings and 'embrace the inner child', but continually subjecting our thoughts, feelings and actions to rigorous self-analysis can result in crippling self-absorption. Instead, we need to be able to observe our feelings with detachment and accept the simple fact that doing a 'bad' thing occasionally does not necessarily make us a 'bad' person.

The middle way between acute self-awareness and self-indulgence is the path of honest appraisal in which we see ourselves as complex human beings acting and reacting to changing circumstances according to our moods, over which we have little control. But if we can't master our moods, we at least need to be able to control our reaction to them otherwise we will be at the mercy of our feelings like a rudderless ship in a storm.

MEDITATE ON YOUR MOODS

To appreciate how fluid your feelings can be, take a few moments to meditate on your feelings at hourly intervals during the day. Recall and describe your emotions during the past hour and the circumstances that gave rise to them. Perhaps you were influenced by someone else's attitude. Could you have reacted differently? Did your reaction intensify the experience? Will you be able to react in a different way if it occurred again?

From now on, become mindful of your moods and learn to consider this mercurial aspect of your personality as a part of what makes you unique.

FEEL THE FEAR

Feel The Fear And Do It Anyway is not only the title of a bestselling self-help book, it is also a good piece

of common sense advice, for the first step towards getting a grip on our fears and phobias is to understand that we are all prey to anxieties of one kind or another and to accept the simple fact what we fear is never as terrible as we imagine it might be. What we really fear is that we might not be up to the challenge. But by worrying at the problem like a dog with a bone we are unwittingly intensifying the experience making our discomfort far worse than the reality of the thing we fear. At such times we will find the inner strength we need in the stillness of meditation.

Whatever is making you apprehensive – whether it is the thought of a job interview or a visit to the dentist – this three-minute meditation will significantly reduce your anxiety.

EXERCISE: BANISHING ANXIETY WITH THE BREATH

- Take a long, deep breath and hold it for a few moments, then let it out as gradually as you can making a soft 'F' sound to expel the last dregs of stale air from your lungs. This will restore your heartbeat to a steady rhythm and reduce the excretion of adrenaline which over stimulates the body, increasing the sense of panic. Repeat this until you feel that you have quietened your mind and clarified your thoughts.

  It is as simple as that.

EXERCISE: A WALK IN THE PARK

- If you still feel anxious, visualise yourself leaving the room and taking a walk around the block. It is a beautiful sunny day and the air is sweet with the scent of cherry blossom and scented flowers. It is still and uncommonly quiet. There is no traffic noise and no one else in sight. It is a public holiday. Everyone is either at the beach, lazing in their gardens or picnicking in the park.

- You decide to walk to the park where you sit down on the grass and listen to the buzzing of the insects, the song of the birds and the sound of children laughing and playing in the distance. Take a long, deep breath of the sweet scented air and feel the warmth of the sun of your face. The perfume of the flowers is intoxicating.

- You can make out the white clothed figures of men playing cricket and children flying their kites. Take your time and take in as many details as you can. You are in no hurry to return. But when you do, sustain this feeling of peace and contentment for as long as you can. Let nothing disturb your stillness and the sense that all is well with the world, your inner world no matter what storms may rage without.

PHOBIAS

Irrational fears and phobias are often symptoms of a deep-rooted anxiety, but once the root cause has been identified they are relatively simple to cure. Again, this visualisation is surprisingly simple, but highly effective.

EXERCISE: STAIRCASE IN THE CLOUDS

1. Close your eyes and focus on your breath. As you inhale say silently to yourself 'calm' and as you exhale say 'and centred'. Repeat this until you are fully relaxed.

2. Now visualise yourself standing at the top of a long winding staircase the bottom of which cannot be seen because it is lost in the clouds far below.

3. When you are ready, begin to walk down, saying the following to yourself as you descend the first steps towards the clouds:

   'Ten ... relax ... Nine ... calm and centred ... Eight ... peaceful and calm ... Seven ... going deeper ... Six ... down ... Five ... deep into relaxation ... Four ... relax ... Three ... down, down ... Two ... deeper ... One ... into the clouds.'

4. As the clouds close around you sense the warmth that comes with deep relaxation and peace of mind. Then pass through the clouds and descend the last steps to the ground saying:

   'Ten ... down ... Nine ... down ... Eight ... deeper ...

Seven ... deeper relaxation ... Six ... letting go all
fears ... Five ... safe and secure ... Four ... safe ...
Three ... and secure ... Two ... safe ... One ...
peace.'

5. You find yourself in the place where your phobia
   originated but you will feel no fear. You are here as
   an observer, interested in resolving this issue but
   detached. In your own words ask your Higher Self,
   your guide or guardian angel to reveal the source
   of this fear for your Highest Good. And when it is
   shown to you ask that it be cleared from your mind
   and your emotional body so that you can evolve
   without fear from now on. If the relevant images
   are not forthcoming, don't despair. They will appear
   in your dreams or come to you in a flash of
   inspiration as the memories are released.

ANGER

Anger could be said to be an expression of our
frustration when we realise that we cannot control
other people or events as we might wish. The only
thing we can control is our anger, but that does not
mean that we have to suppress such emotions or
condemn ourselves for occasionally giving in to what
is a natural human reaction. The following exercise
impresses the danger of irrational and intense rage on
the unconscious mind so that your immediate reaction

in the future will be to control your temper and channel your anger into a constructive physical activity such as washing the car, clearing the clutter from your home or digging the garden.

EXERCISE: THE FAMILY PHOTO

1. Imagine you are holding a treasured photo of your family and friends standing outside your home. Or you might prefer to substitute a photo of a favourite pet or possession.

2. Now allow your anger to arise as you recall the situation that has brought on these feelings. Become acutely aware of the emotion as a burning sensation in the pit of your stomach and feel it rising up through your chest, along your arms and into your fingers.

If you don't extinguish this fire in a moment it will consume whatever you hold dear. Is it worth indulging your anger at such a cost? Before the flames reach the photograph plunge your hands into an imaginary basin of cool water and extinguish the fire.

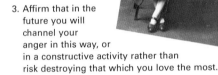

3. Affirm that in the future you will channel your anger in this way, or in a constructive activity rather than risk destroying that which you love the most.

COPING WITH LOSS

There are many forms of loss. The death of a parent, partner, child, relative or close friend is, of course, the main form of bereavement, but to the person who is suffering the break up of a long term relationship, divorce or even redundancy can be just as intense and painful an experience.

There is no cure for grief, but meditation can help the bereaved to accept the loss as being part of the natural process of life and death and it can also enable them to complete the vital final act of 'letting go'.

It must be pointed out, however, that in cases where there is trauma or serious emotional disturbance it is not advisable to do the following meditation as it can have a profound effect on an unbalanced psyche. In such cases where the grief is intensely painful the only suitable meditations are the most basic calming, grounding and centering exercises described in the earlier chapters.

EXERCISE: THE EMPTY CHAIR

1. Make yourself comfortable, close your eyes and allow yourself to sink into a state of deep relaxation.

2. When you are ready, visualise yourself sitting opposite an empty chair. Now ask for your guide or guardian angel to appear behind you and sense its comforting presence. Feel the protection of its wings

or hands upon your shoulders and know that you are protected and at peace.

3. Now imagine that the person you wish to say goodbye to gradually appears in the empty chair with their guide or guardian angel behind them in the shadows.

4. Say whatever you want, whether it is asking forgiveness, expressing your love for them, or simply saying goodbye in your own way. If you are ending a relationship it is a good idea to sever your emotional ties to them by imagining that you are cutting the strands that link your heart chakra to theirs. It can also be beneficial for your own peace of mind and emotional wellbeing to wish them well in life and to affirm in words of your own choosing that there is no longer any obligation between you. If you find this difficult at first, persevere and it will become easier in subsequent meditations.

EXERCISE: LETTING GO

1. Close your eyes and imagine the person you loved emerging from a luminous cloud, radiant with the life force that is the essence of their being. See them as they were when they were at their happiest. This is particularly important when

it is a person who has died after a long and debilitating illness as you need to impress a positive image in your memory so that you will always associate them with happier times and leave all feelings of guilt and regret behind.

2. Now reach out and embrace them. Tell them how much you loved them, that you miss them, but that you have to let them go. You need to move on with your life now so that you can experience whatever it is that you have to learn from this incarnation,

while they need rest and time to assimilate what they have learnt from this life. If there is anything that you need to resolve, clear it now and be done with it. Perhaps you want to give them something to remember you by and they may do the same. Let the image of this object arise spontaneously and leave the analysis of its significance until after the meditation.

3. Now say goodbye and watch as they return to the light in peace. Affirm that there is no emotional residue on either side other than love. Then return to waking consciousness.

Mind Matters

STRESS RELIEF

The ultimate aim of meditation is enlightenment and the first goal is peace of mind. Stress can be a useful ally in attaining goals and driving us to fulfil our ambitions, but there is a danger of it becoming addictive and affecting our health and relationships. We therefore need to find a middle way between activity and relaxation, a state of mind the Buddhists call being in the world but not of it. The following exercises aim to create that balance.

EXERCISE:
DRIFTING ON A CLOUD

1. Lie on a bed or mat with your head supported by a cushion. Keep your arms by your sides and your legs slightly apart parallel with your shoulders.

2. Focus on your breath, then scan your body for tension beginning with your toes. Tighten each muscle in turn, hold that for a moment, and then relax.

3. Now begin to build a bolster of energy under your body with each exhalation and feel yourself becoming detached from your physical body, but remain acutely aware of your surroundings. As this cushion of air takes form it begins rising

gently, carrying you up through the ceiling and out of the house, on and up into the cloudless sky.

4. Look down and see the turning earth far below, the roads and houses, the hills, fields and the coast in the distance. Enjoy the feeling of weightlessness, the warm, soft breeze on your face and the liberating sensation as you float freely on the gentle current of air. While you are in this state of deep relaxation consider what might the source of stress in your life and how you might be free of it.

5. When you are ready to return, drift back down to earth, become aware once again of your surroundings and sense the weight of your body on the bed. Then open your eyes.

WORRY

If you find it difficult to relax and have trouble sleeping you need to identify the source of your anxieties and put them into perspective. This visualisation should help you to do both.

EXERCISE: THE RAFT

1. Imagine that you are about to go on a river journey and are carrying most of your belongings in a small raft. The raft is tied to the quayside by a rope. Is it thick, strong and secure or could the raft come

adrift in a strong wind? Are you eager to leave and discover new sights or are you reluctant to leave something behind and guilty at the thought of having time for yourself? If you are reluctant to leave, what is it that is holding you back?

2. Whatever your feelings are it is now time to cast off and drift with the current. Take a last look at the quayside as you leave the safety of the shore. What and who do you see there? What are your feelings at this moment?

3. At first you make steady progress, but then the weight of your belongings slows the raft and makes navigation difficult. You are rapidly

approaching a dangerous fast flowing turn in the river. What do you throw overboard to save yourself?

4. You succeed in overcoming the obstacles, but a moment later you hit the rocks and the raft overturns. You can only save one thing. What is it? You swim to the shore with this precious possession and rest before making your way back home.

5. Now become aware of your surroundings and open your eyes.

DEPRESSION

Depression is a state of mind and often has no basis in reality, although it can also be triggered by physical processes in the body (eg., postnatal depression). It is an emotional response to an irrational belief that we are not in control of our lives and so cannot influence events. But we have free will and if we choose to exercise it we can create own reality.

EXERCISE

- The next time you are feeling depressed relax into a meditative state and recall a happy scene from your childhood. Even if you have had a difficult childhood there will be a pleasant memory to recall. Then think of a happy time in your

adolescence and finally, another enjoyable day from adulthood.

- Next, recall a time in your childhood you were in some kind of difficulty or danger and were saved from injury by what at the time seemed to be good luck or a fortunate intervention by someone else. Then recall a similar incident in your teenage years and finally, in adulthood. Could it be that someone or something was watching over you and that you are not alone in life as you might imagine?

- Close the meditation by choosing a piece of music from your tape or CD collection that sums up how you feel when you are depressed and play it, then

another that expresses a more positive outlook and
play that. Finally, pick a piece of music that
expresses how you would like to feel and which
seems to say that all is right with the world. You
might consider recording these pieces so that you
can play yourself out of depression the next time
you feel down.

ADDICTION

The common definition of addiction involves
dependence on something that artificially stimulates
the senses (be it drugs, alcohol, food or even fast
cars), but a crucial part of the problem is the addict's
willingness to empower an inanimate object or
substance with the ability to control their lives.

The following visualisation is intended to supplement
professional medical treatment for the more serious
forms of addiction, not replace it.

EXERCISE

1. Make yourself comfortable, close your eyes and
   imagine that the object of your addiction is within
   your reach. You can touch it but you don't need to
   at the moment. You decide when you want it and
   you don't want it now.

2. You resent being dependent upon it and the things

that it has taken from you. You resent it for the effect it has had on your health, the precious time wasted on it when you could have been with your friends and family, time that you will never have again. You resent it for the money that you have wasted on it, for depriving you of your love for life and for making you intense and unhappy. But most of all you resent it for making you believe that you have no freewill. You do have freewill and you are going to prove it by putting this detested substance or object where it belongs.

3. Put it in a box, lock it and place the key out of reach. Now push it away from you or better still, drop it in the dustbin and affirm your determination to be free from its influence. Don't think that you're wasting it by disposing of it. It is better

to dump it than allow it to undermine your self-respect or to disturb your peace of mind.

4. Now visualise yourself leaving the room and taking a walk around the block. Enjoy the fresh air and your new found freedom.

PROSPERITY PROGRAMMING

Our income and quality of life is not always a direct result of hard work or of our share of life's lucky breaks. Some people don't seem to get their share no matter how conscientious and hard working they might be and it is often because unconsciously they

PROSPERITY PROGRAMMING: AFFIRMATIONS

- 'This is an abundant universe and there is plenty for everyone.'

- 'Everything I need is coming to me effortlessly right now.'

- 'The universe always provides.'

- 'Money flows to me and I am ready to receive what is right for me.'

don't feel that they deserve it. Maybe they believe
that it is wrong to have money when others are poor,
or that if they spend it there won't be any more to
replace it, so they don't attract wealth, or they
contrive to let it run through their fingers like grains
of sand.

EXERCISE

- If you have difficulty attracting wealth or holding
  onto it choose one of the affirmations on page 163
  and meditate on it. Allow your thoughts and
  impressions to bubble up from the unconscious
  and then analyse them afterwards to identify what
  is preventing you from creating abundance and a
  better quality of life.

GUILT

Guilt serves no purpose as it is a form of self
punishment for an action or omission that is in the
past and therefore cannot be changed. We have to
accept that we all make mistakes and that we do so
to learn from them. As long as we have resolved not
to make the same mistake again, we should forgive
ourselves and move forward, otherwise we relive the
same experience again and again to no useful
purpose.

EXERCISE:
THE THEATRE

- Relax into meditation and when you are ready, visualise yourself sitting in the front row of a small theatre. The lights are down and you are quite alone.

- Then the curtain rises on a familiar scene. The setting is the same as that in which you made what you consider to be your big 'mistake'. You watch with interest as anonymous actors recreate the events and speak the precise words that you and the other party or parties spoke. Does this give you a new perspective on the situation?

- Consider the fact that real life is not scripted and so you can't foresee events or how other people might react, especially when there is a misunderstanding. You can't always have a ready and intelligent answer when you're unexpectedly put on the spot, neither can you be expected to send everyone home happy when the curtain falls with all the loose ends tied up as does the playwright who has invented the roles and is manipulating the characters. You are not following someone else's stage directions you are improvising the scenes from your life as you go along.

- Now bring the curtain down on this particular scene and be done with it.

The Higher Self

SEEKING GUIDANCE

Imagine how wonderful it would be to be able to turn to a wise, compassionate and understanding friend whenever you needed comfort and advice; someone who knows you better than you do yourself and who always has your best interests at heart. Well, you can.

Through meditation you can open a channel to the source of intuition, inspiration and insight which psychologists call the Unconscious, but which those on the spiritual path call the Higher-Self.

EXERCISE: CREATING AN INNER SANCTUARY

To establish contact with your inner guide you need to create a receptive state of mind and this is done by creating an inner sanctuary through visualisation.

This sacred space is usually envisaged as a garden, as this is a universal symbol of peace and also a boundary between the lower and upper worlds of matter and spirit.

1. When you are in a state of deep relaxation, visualise yourself standing by the entrance to a walled garden. The door or gate is over-grown with briars so you need to cut or pull them away before you can enter. What do

you find inside? Is the garden neglected as the entrance suggested, or has it been well-tended as if awaiting your return?

2. You immediately begin sweeping leaves from the paths and clearing the flower beds of weeds. Then prune the bushes and trees of deadwood to encourage new growth. If you discover any furniture or features take time to restore them before making a bonfire and burning the rubbish. But remember, this is a labour of love and should not be hurried. The more care you put into renovating this place, the greater the pleasure you will have when you visit it in search of peace.

3. When your work is done, rest and take satisfaction from your efforts.

EXERCISE: MEETING YOUR INNER GUIDE

Once your inner sanctuary is established you can visit it anytime that you need guidance or when you need space for yourself after a demanding day.

1. Relax into meditation and visualise yourself entering the walled garden again. There is a fountain in the centre. Sit down on the grass beside it, listen to the bubbling waters of the fountain and look into the calm surface of the water.

2. There is a spot of reflected sunlight in the water which fixes you with its brilliance. As you continue to stare at it the light begins to intensify, but it doesn't hurt your eyes. As you look into the light a figure can be seen in the centre. The light now envelops you and the figure emerges appearing before you in the garden.

3. You have no fear. The figure is your inner guide. It has a kindly face radiant with unconditional love and compassion. In its eyes you have done nothing wrong. What you considered to be mistakes, it saw only as opportunities to learn and understand the human condition.

4. Now ask whatever questions come to your mind and listen for the answers. Spend time in the company of your guide taking strength from his or her presence and absorbing the energy that he shares with you.

5. After you return to waking consciousness don't rush back to your usual routine. Sit still and try to sustain the sense of serenity that you felt in that sacred space.

PATHWORKING

Once you have established an inner sanctuary and met with your guide you might want to go deeper into the uncharted regions of the unconscious. If so, the next logical step is Pathworking, which takes its name from the 22 paths linking the Sephirah on the Kabbalisitic Tree Of Life (see p. 98). This is a specialised form of visualisation in which you can explore the inner landscape of your psyche in symbolic form. For example, if you have difficulties making an important decision because your emotions are always clouding the issue, you could visualise a scene in which you

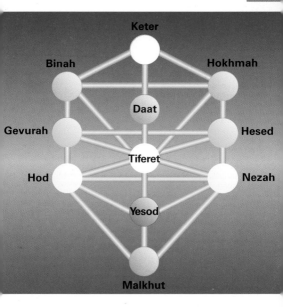

focus on the rational and logical aspect of your personality (represented by a specific sphere on the Tree). Once you have emphasised this dispassionate quality, you can then bring it to another scene symbolic of your emotions. By becoming acutely aware of your mental and emotional makeup in this way you will be able to identify any imbalance in your personality and prevent one attribute dominating at the expense of another.

It might be easier to understand if you consider the consequences of an imbalance between the complimentary characteristics of Judgement and Mercy. If an individual was predisposed to being judgemental they might be self-critical to the point where they couldn't find satisfaction in anything that they had achieved and had little compassion for others. If, on the other hand, they overindulged the compassionate side of their nature they might lack drive and a competitive edge.

The principle can even be projected into the wider world as all communities, from individual families to entire nations, have what is known as a group soul.

When these same qualities are out of balance in a particular state it will manifest either as a strict, draconian regime or as a liberal judicial system which is too lenient on criminals.

To take the first step into the inner landscape of your own psyche try the following visualisation. When you are ready to explore the other attributes on the Tree Of Life you will need an introductory guide to Kabbalah or a book devoted exclusively to Pathworking.

EXERCISE:
THE TEMPLE OF HOD

- Begin by visualising yourself standing at the entrance to a temple. This is the temple of Malkhut (The Kingdom) which represents our physical world, the starting point of every inner journey. The door is flanked by two massive pillars symbolising the governing principles of the universe, Form and Force.

- You enter and find yourself in a sparse vaulted chamber lit by four tall candles, one in each corner to mark the four cardinal points (north, south, east and west). As your eyes adjust to the light you notice that the temple has a chequered floor representing the duality of existence and you are facing a simple stone altar on which have been placed traditional symbols of the four elements of fire, air, earth and water: a sword, a rod and a chalice with water.

- Behind the altar you can make out three exits over which are draped curtains embroidered with images taken from the Tarot trumps (the picture cards of the major arcana). To your left is the Wheel of Fortune representing the cycle of death and rebirth and the law of karma (the universal law of cause and effect). On the central curtain is the image of the World representing discrimination, experience and fulfilment and to the right is a depiction of The Fool representing self-determination and individual freewill.

- On this occasion you choose to pass through the curtain to your left and find yourself in a corridor lined with images depicting scenes from your past lives. Allow the images to arise spontaneously and do not be tempted to analyse or judge what you see. Each incarnation expressed just a facet of your Higher Self, the totality of which can only be glimpsed after a multitude of lifetimes.

- At the end of the corridor you are faced with another door. You may find that the way is barred by the appropriate archetype (see below), in this case a muscular figure representing the physical world. If so, ask for permission to pass.

- Enter the inner chamber of Hod, the sphere corresponding to the intellect, specifically communication and learning. You could visualise it as a study or library. Here you may encounter the relevant archetype who personifies these characteristics, a receptive and enthusiastic student who will be willing to offer you guidance and insight in these matters. Maybe you need to be more self-disciplined, or perhaps you find it difficult to express yourself clearly. Here you will find the answers you seek.

- When you are ready, you can either return the way you came or explore other areas using the following key to the spheres.

KEY TO THE SPHERES

MALKHUT
(THE KINGDOM)

The physical realm in which your ideas and aspirations are brought into manifest existence. In meditation on this aspect of your personality use house and garden settings to stay grounded.

YESOD (THE FOUNDATION)

The realm of the ego. This is the place to examine how you perceive the world and your self-image. Visualise a room of mirrors, or a tower with a window on the world below. Another suitable setting would be a room in which you have collected momentos and photographs of your life.

HOD (REVERBERATION)

A library or study setting will help focus your mind on your intellectual attributes.

NEZAH (ETERNITY)

A sensual garden or fairground is an ideal setting to explore your attitude to pleasure.

TIFERET (BEAUTY)

The centre of unconditional love and compassion as envisaged by your guardian angel, a spiritual being of your choice such as Jesus or Buddha or the Higher Self.

GEVURAH (JUDGMENT)

A celestial court might be ideal for considering the laws and rules that you have chosen to live under and enforce upon yourself and others.

HESED (MERCY)

Again, a court would seem the most suitable setting. Imagine yourself in the role of a defence council pleading mitigating circumstance in your own defence.

It can be a very enlightening and salutary experience.

DAAT (HIGHER KNOWLEDGE)

This is the one unmanifest sephiroth on the Tree and as such may be envisaged as a bridge to be crossed or a dark tunnel. Traditionally this point in the journey towards self-awareness has been represented by the hero's battle with a giant, dragon or demon symbolising their own shadow self.

BINAH (UNDERSTANDING)

Imagine confiding in a compassionate teacher or guru.

HOKHMAH (WISDOM)

Imagine that you have been granted a private audience with a true prophet or oracle who can see your future and can reveal to you your True Nature.

KETER (THE CROWN)

Enter the inner chamber and secure the treasure that awaits you at the end of your quest.

ARCHETYPES

When you explore the psyche using symbolic images in this way you may meet archetypal figures whose appearance indicates that you are on the right path.

From a psychological viewpoint they can be seen as
representing the various complementary aspects of the
persona, while on a spiritual level they are symbolic of
the stages of our ascent to self-realisation or
perfection.

*MALKHUT
(THE KINGDOM)*

The naked form of a strong, healthy man or woman
representing the physical world.

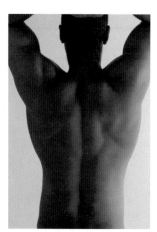

*YESOD (THE
FOUNDATION)*

An ambitious
prince or gifted
and wilful child
representing the
ego.

*HOD
(REVERBERATION)*

A receptive and
enthusiastic
student
representing the
active aspect of
our natural

intelligence concerned with communication and learning.

NEZAH (ETERNITY)

A sensual figure representing the instincts and the preoccupation with pleasure and pain.

TIFERET (BEAUTY)

An angel representing the Higher Self.

GEVURAH (JUDGMENT)

A learned authority figure representing self-discipline, decisiveness and discernment.

HESED (MERCY)

A maternal figure representing tolerance, unconditional love and forgiveness.

DAAT (HIGHER KNOWLEDGE)

A composer or artist deep in thought representing inspiration and intuition. This is not strictly an archetype, rather an unmanifest attribute, a chasm we have to cross from worldly awareness to enlightenment.

BINAH (UNDERSTANDING)

A learned, compassionate and patient teacher whose uncommon understanding is the result of long study and reflection.

HOKHMAH (WISDOM)

A prophet or mystic whose glimpse of the greater reality represents revelation.

KETER (THE CROWN)

The sun or a radiant star representing the divine aspect of human nature.

EXERCISE: HALL OF LIFE

1. Make yourself comfortable, close your eyes and

focus on your breath. Take slow deep regular
breaths.

2. Imagine that it is night and that you are alone
   outside in a strangely familiar landscape.

3. You are standing at the entrance to what appears
   to be a museum or library of some sort. There is a
   light in one of the windows, but no one seems to
   be inside. You try the door and find it unlocked. To
   your pleasant surprise you find yourself in a
   spacious entrance hall facing a large notice which
   reads 'Today's Exhibition: The Life of..' In the space
   is your own name.

4. You walk through into the first gallery which is
   labelled 'Part One'. Here is preserved every
   incident in your life so far. Every minute detail,
   every thought and every spoken word. Every
   action and every reaction preserved in tableus and
   on film. Not for judging, but rather for detached
   observation so that all those who visit here can
   learn about how the spirit fares in the physical
   world. The most significant episodes, positive and
   negative as we would see them, are set aside as
   tableus in glass cabinets or sculpted in stone and
   arranged on plinths in alcoves with the relevant
   dates.

5. You survey the achievements of your life so far

with justifiable pride and note the less positive aspects as moments to learn from. There are displays where you can once again experience the sights, sounds and sensations of your happiest memories if you choose to do so. Do not be afraid to re-screen these as they cannot harm you now. You are a detached observer of your own life.

6. As you come to the closed doors at the end of this first gallery marked with an exit sign you pause and reflect on what you have seen, on

the pattern of your life which is now becoming apparent to you as it had not done so before. Just as you are about to leave you notice an open book set upon a lectern, a stand, to one side. You glance across to it and see what is written there. It might be a comment on your past actions or advice for the future.

7. You open the door and pass through into a small lobby entrance or hallway. Across the way is another set of doors over which is a sign. It says 'Part Two'. You have created the exhibitions on display in the first gallery. Now what would you like to find inside if you were allowed to continue into the second? You try the doors but they are locked. So noticing a side exit you pass through it instead and emerge outside in the still, warm night air under the stars.

8. Now open your eyes and make a note of all that you have seen and end with a note concerning what you would like to achieve in the second part of your life.

PROCESS OF CREATION

The ultimate aim of meditation is Enlightenment, the realisation and intuitive understanding that there is a unity and purpose to existence. The following exercise is believed to have been practised by followers of the western esoteric tradition since biblical times and though it appears simple it can have a profound and enlight-ening effect. So ground yourself well before you undertake the ultimate journey. (See Grounding, p. 00.)

EXERCISE

1. Visualise yourself at the entrance to a mountain, the interior of which is lit by flaming torches. Take one of the torches and begin your descent into the centre of the earth past multi-coloured strata of rock and minerals embedded with fossils from the ages before man walked on our planet.

2. When you reach the centre of the earth you come

upon the bubbling molten core from which new mountains and land masses will be formed. This is the prima matter of new life, the process creation made manifest. Now follow the stream of molten rock through a fissure in the mountain side and emerge into the dark at the bottom of the ocean.

3. Now begin your ascent to the surface through the myriad forms of aquatic life whose variety of forms is a marvel to behold.

4. You emerge on a white sandy beach, but instead of walking along the shore you continue to rise upwards taking flight with the seabirds. Watch the coast receding below you as you float upwards towards the clouds. From here you drift over villages, towns and cities observing their inhabitants. See babies being born into the world, the young seeking knowledge, the middle-aged assimilating experience, the elderly coming to an understanding of life and those who are ready to return to the realm of spirit accepting the embrace of an angel's wings. Look down on the turning earth below teeming with life, nourished by the blue waters of the oceans, rivers, lakes and streams and by the warmth of the sun.

5. Now ascend through the black silence of space to a point of light beyond the last star in the universe.

As you draw near you can see that it is a tunnel of light beyond which is the world of spirit. You are drawn to the light at the end of the tunnel by an irresistible force. It is unconditional Love. At the end of the tunnel you are embraced by this force in the form of a spiritual being. Your long journey is now at an end. Ask what you will and it will be granted. Perhaps you need healing, guidance or simply the Love that is yours by right as a divine being.

6. When you are ready, begin your descent back though the tunnel of light until you find yourself gazing down on the turning earth below. Become aware of your surroundings, the weight of your body and then open your eyes.

BIBLIOGRAPHY

Gawain, S *Creative Visualisation* New World Library, California, 1978

Hillman, J *The Soul's Code* Bantam, New York, 1996

Millman, D *Everyday Enlightenment* Hodder & Stoughton, London, 1998

Rinpoche, S *The Tibetan Book Of Days* Ebury, London, 1993

Roland, P *How To Meditate* Octopus/Hamlyn, London, 2001

Roland, P *Meditation Solutions* Octopus/Hamlyn, London, 2002

Shine, B *Mind To Mind* Corgi, London, 1996

Shine, B *Mind Workbook* Corgi, London, 1997

Roland, P *Kabbalah: A Piatkus Guide* Piatkus, London, 1999

WEBSITES

The websites listed below are examples of those that can be found on the internet. There are hundreds of others which can be accessed by through search engines such as www.google.com.

www.wccm.org

www.meditationcenter.com

www.tm.org

www.learningmeditation.com

www.meditationweb.com